BARBARISM IN GREECE

A young American lawyer's inquiry
into the use of torture
in contemporary Greece,
with case histories and documents

By JAMES BECKET

Foreword by SENATOR CLAIBORNE PELL

WALKER AND COMPANY • New York

First published in the United States of America in 1970 by the Walker Publishing Company, Inc.

Published simultaneously in Canada by The Ryerson Press, Toronto.

Library of Congress Catalog Card Number: 73-109187

Printed in the United States of America

Book designed by Lena Fong Hor

TABLE OF CONTENTS

To Greeks who care about democracy
To democrats who care about Greece

FOREWORD

by *Claiborne Pell, United States Senator*

Greece is the cradle of Western civilization: freedom and democracy were nurtured in Greece, and many of the qualities that make ours a better life originated there. These qualities have prevailed in Greece despite hundreds of years of travail and of occupation by the Ottoman empire.

Now, suddenly, the vitality of Greece—her gregarious public spirit —has been cruelly blanketed by the present junta.

As one who has traveled in Greece, who loves that country and its people, I have spoken often on the Floor of the Senate on the contrasts between the freedom and independence that was Greece's and the cruel regime that now dominates that country.

In following the grotesque happenings in Greece since the junta took over, I have been particularly impressed by the work of Amnesty International and men like James Becket, who almost without thought of personal sacrifice or risk, have done what they could to alleviate the unhappy lot of the junta's prisoners.

The Council of Europe has confirmed the allegations that I have been making on the Senate Floor to the effect that the Greek regime has countenanced the use of torture as a matter of administrative practice to extract information from prisoners and to discourage men and women from engaging in any activity unsympathetic to the junta regime.

I regret to say that so far I have found myself in a minority when it comes to doing something about my concern. In fact, there is an all too general acceptance of the view that, bad as the junta may be, we need the use of the Greek facilities for NATO. The Pentagon seems to approve of the Greek government as an efficient government and one which provides agreeable ports of call for our military forces. The executive branch of our government, as a whole, has a "no-policy" policy. Our Senate is divided on this issue, as shown by its 45–38 vote knocking out my amendment that would have terminated military assistance to the Greek junta. Yet, our people, I believe, have a justified revulsion to the Greek regime.

For this reason, I wish good luck to James Becket and to Amnesty International for all they are doing to improve the lot of the unfortunate people in Greece who wish to restore individualism and freedom to their beloved country.

PREFACE

This is basically a book of documents. Some are reports of international organizations, others are statements of governments, and the majority are the affidavits of Greeks describing their experiences in the hands of the Greek authorities. All of them deal with one theme—torture in the Greece of the Colonels. A short time ago, I never would have imagined that I would be putting this book together.

In late December of 1967 I was sent to Greece by Amnesty International of London and since then I have been deeply involved with this subject. There I first had contact with human beings who have been tortured. For an American brought up in the sheltered environment of a New England village, belonging to the silent generation between Korea and Viet Nam, this was a profound shock. I am sometimes asked why I got so involved with this question. Though I am not always so sure why I got involved in general, the reason it was Greece in particular is easily explained. I married a Greek.

After our marriage in 1960 my wife and I often went to Greece for summer vacation, attracted by the sea and the sun, the same elements that have always attracted tourists to that beautiful country. In 1967, three months after the Colonels came to power, we went again to the small village where we went each summer. It was not the same. In the cemetery was the grave of a young woman who had been shot by a soldier on the day of the coup; a man from the village had been taken to prison; and all the elected officials had been dismissed. Most of all there was fear—it was only after ten days that any of our friends dared to speak about the political situation.

In December of 1967, Amnesty International, a humanitarian organization dedicated to helping those imprisoned for their ideas, contacted me about going on a mission to Greece with a British lawyer. They asked me because I knew Greece, could speak some Greek, and was a lawyer. I agreed to go. On December 23rd, the regime announced "an amnesty," but it proved to be a cruel hoax, especially at Christmastime, since only a handful of the more than four thousand political prisoners was released. It did, however, give a starting point from which to approach the government. I made the first of these trips to Greece not for the sun and not for the sea.

Arriving in Athens on December 30th, I met my British colleague, Anthony Marreco, a lawyer who had participated in the Nuremberg Trials. He was to deal with the government, while I was to gather information from private sources. Our basic task was to find out who the political prisoners were, where they were being held, and why they were being held. Little did we know that while we spent a quiet New Year's Eve in our hotel, Greeks were being tortured, and in the same city a motorcycle engine on the roof terrace of the Bouboulinas St. Security Police Headquarters was drowning out the cries of victims. Athens was an appropriate place to greet 1968, Human Rights Year.

It was not easy, especially for someone who knew Athens from before, to adjust to the new reality. To call only from a kiosk. To always look behind. To visit only when the concierge is asleep. To change taxis. To be afraid. In our era of spy spoofs and James Bond, you begin by feeling rather ridiculous, but in time you take it seriously, especially when you realize your passport protects you, but not the person who had the courage to meet you.

In our search for information about prisoners, we began to hear tales of torture, but they were always secondhand—that is, hearsay. It was only after ten days that a victim finally dared to speak to us, and only after the rendezvous had been carefully arranged in a safe place. She was a young woman. At that time perhaps we did not fully appreciate the great courage it took for her to speak to two strangers. For someone who has been tortured, the only fate worse than death is the prospect of being tortured again, and that is exactly what those who were released were threatened with if they ever said a word to anyone about their experiences. We had hoped, rather naïvely, that torture victims would sign an affidavit to be kept with a reliable person abroad who could swear it was signed. But one look into this woman's eyes and any legalistic demands on her suffering were out of the question. She spoke only on the condition that we not know her name. She was as many others would be: her hands shook, she chainsmoked and she started at each sound from outside the room. At times in her story she broke down completely. Her account of her experiences is in this book. What was most convincing about the many victims I was later to see—aside from the scars I saw—was how they were as human beings—they were mentally and physically shattered.

I saw more than twenty persons, and wrote down each of their stories on a piece of paper, designating the "case" only with a number. My stomach was to stay in a knot that whole month in Greece. It was the sheer injustice of so many cases that was most ulcerous. People had been mercilessly tortured simply for being in possession of a leaflet criticizing the regime. Brutality and cruelty on one side, frustration and helplessness on the other. They were being tortured and there was nothing to be done. It was like listening to a friend who has cancer. What comfort, what wise reflection can someone who is comfortable give? Torture might last a short time, but the person will never be the same.

My briefcase was filling with cases and I was growing increasingly anxious. Outside our apartment, loitering on the corner, were three heavy-set men in trenchcoats looking everywhere but at us. I managed to send out the case histories in a safe way, but still had material that could compromise my informants. I had a list of the names of thirty-two tortured persons which I had obtained from secondhand sources, such as the families, lawyers, and fellow prisoners. I put it in my toothpaste tube. I was scared the day we went to the airport, but we passed without incident and soon were again in a free country.

Upon our return we wrote a report for Amnesty, which is included in this book. This report was widely circulated and, though we had gone to Greece with no intention of investigating torture, it was this part of the report that received the most attention in the press. Yet still the fact that torture was practiced in Greece was not generally accepted. After all, we were not able to produce names. And it is a long way from the few isolated cases of police brutality that happen in every country to a deliberate government policy to torture. The government promptly attacked the report as "malicious lying," and the Greek press called us "homosexuals" and "Communists." The battle was not over just because a few foreigners had spoken with some victims and were convinced. The battle, in fact, was just beginning.

The question then was to get help from those institutions that could do something about stopping the torture. The International Committee of the Red Cross had a presence in Greece and had permission to visit political detainees, but they were sceptical and unresponsive on the issue of torture. It was to be hoped that the U.S. government with its dominant influence in Greece could do something about it. My mother, in Connecticut, started a campaign writing letters to Congressmen and anyone who might help on this issue. The official answers from the State Department made clear to us the position of the U.S. government toward the junta. The torture question was one about which we knew certain facts, though presumably fewer than the U.S. government with its large Embassy staff and intelligence services. Yet the letters that came back about torture were uniformly defensive, citing only sources that would disclaim the practice, and containing misrepresentations that would mislead the uninformed reader. We realized that in the battle to make known to people what was going on in the police stations and army camps of Greece, Greeks could not, to put it charitably, count on the considerable resources of the State Department and other less visible branches of the U.S. government. The more research I did on this question, the more apparent it became that the U.S. government's involvement in torture went beyond simply moral support. It is only in the U.S. Congress that the Greek people have found any allies, notably Senator Claiborne Pell, who are willing to raise their voices on this issue.

There is, however, an institution specifically designed for the problem—the European Commission of Human Rights. The democratic European countries of the Council of Europe have signed the European Convention of Human Rights, which empowers the Commission to investigate violations. Article Three of the Convention expressly forbids torture. In March I met Mr. Jens Evensen, the head of the Legal Department of the Norwegian Foreign Office, who was the Chief Agent of the Scandinavian countries in their case against the Greek government which they brought in September of 1967. They had not included torture then as one of the articles of the Convention which Greece had violated, but now they wanted to add it to their application before the Commission. He was looking for evidence. At that point there were few names. Almost every day since I had left Greece, however, word arrived of new torture cases, new pleas for help, new tragedies. Yet still the names could not be made public and if they were presented to the Commission they would automatically be made available to the Greek government.

Gradually the problem of names was solved. Mr. Marreco made another trip to Greece, which is described elsewhere in the book, and this time nine tortured prisoners had the remarkable courage to allow their names to be publicly used. The junta was now clearly worried over the torture issue and they counterattacked through official denials, through Red Cross reports, and through public relations firms hired abroad. In the spring of 1968 the first torture victim escaped from Greece, but she could not speak as she still had a brother in the army in Greece. In July the first Greek spoke about his torture before a court-martial. The dossier was growing more ample as the first Commission hearings scheduled for November in Strasbourg approached. The tragedy was that with each day that passed more Greeks were being tortured.

In September I flew to Greece to write an article on the referendum on the constitution. I also hoped during this trip to get more names and information on the torture question. After landing at the airport, I was stopped at the passport control. I spent four hours in a small office of the security police there at the airport. I was not allowed to telephone the American Embassy nor make any other communication, and was even accompanied to the toilet by a security policeman. Since I knew the names of so many of their colleagues who were torturers, we at least had a topic of conversation. I was never given any reason for being refused entry into Greece, though it could only have been because of the Amnesty Report. A plainclothesman escorted me all the way to the door of the plane leaving for Rome.

On November 25th the first hearings on torture opened before a sub-Commission in Strasbourg. Here there was the atmosphere of a court where every allegation had to be proved beyond any doubt. The Scandinavians had only one witness who had actually been tortured; the rest, like me, had but a secondhand knowledge and in most cases were bound by promises not to reveal names. The evidence that could be given seemed meager. A highly dramatic week began with two junta witnesses who had been tortured escaping from their hotel to defect to our side. These events are described in the case of Constantine Meletis. The Scandinavian case looked stronger as the week progressed, and there was reason to be optimistic. At the same time my wife and I realized that there might be personal danger for us. The French police warned her not to travel alone. In the ensuing months my wife was accosted twice outside our apartment and warned by a Greek, "You are playing with fire at Strasbourg! "

At the December hearing, there were no witnesses who had been tortured, and this lack was a serious problem for the Scandinavians. The Commission was preparing to go to Greece in February, but no one was sure that witnesses would dare to speak. Already the police were calling in those victims who had been released to make them sign papers that they had been well treated. The Greek resistance helped victims escape from Greece, and refugees began to appear at our door often after harrowing experiences. They testified at the spring hearings of the sub-Commission.

Articles about torture had appeared in the European press, but it was not well covered in America until an article in the *Look* issue of May 27, 1969, "Greece: Government by Torture." We were as pleased about this article as Prime Minister Papadopoulos was displeased. On June 8, 1969, he challenged the author of the article and "the person who supplied the information" to come to Greece to make an "objective investigation." *Look* answered the challenge, naming the writer Christopher Wren, Congressman Don Edwards of California, and me, to go for this investigation. For a while I thought I might get back to sunny Greece, but when the Greek government finally gave an answer, it was that we three were "totally unacceptable" and would not be welcome.

The reaction to the *Look* article, especially in America showed that many people and organizations were not convinced. In my files there were hundreds of names, scores of affidavits, and innumerable documents. I felt an obligation to make this evidence public.

The subject of this book is horrible. Torture belongs on the darkest side of human behavior, yet in the Greek case there are entries to be made on the credit side of the human ledger. People outside of Greece, especially in Europe, have cared about what was going on, and public opinion has played a role. The European Press has vigorously pursued the subject. The international community through its organizations has shown that it is willing to try to do something about it. The Scandinavian governments brought their case before the European Commission of Human Rights not for any commercial or territorial advantage, but because they believed in human rights. Despite pressure from many sides, they had the perseverance to see the case through to its conclusion. The members of the Commission conscientiously discharged their duty, concluding that the Greek regime tortures political prisoners as a matter of policy. Most important of all, Greeks themselves, at great personal sacrifice, had the courage to tell their stories and give their names.

I am convinced that because of this fewer Greeks have been tortured than would have been if the regime had a free hand. Efforts from abroad, however, have their limits, which are tragically demonstrated by the fact the regime continues to torture prisoners. In a sense the possible international effort has now been made, and torture has not been stopped. The future is uncertain. All that has happened, all that is described in these pages cannot be simply forgotten by Greeks. If there is not a change soon, it is difficult to see how Greece can avoid great bloodshed.

December, 1969

INTRODUCTION

On April 21, 1967, a group of military officers carried out a successful coup d'etat in Greece. It was the first such coup in Europe since the Second World War. Instead of the elections that had been scheduled for May, there were mass arrests, purges, martial law, censorship—all the familiar features of a military dictatorship. The new regime justified such measures by equally familiar declarations that it was saving the nation from a "communist takeover." Of all the practices of the regime which violate human rights, none has caused more controversy than the use of torture. The regime firmly maintains that torture has not been used, while others claim that the victims number in the thousands.

While an attempt can be made to justify the violation of certain human rights on the grounds of necessity or ideology, the generally accepted values of our time permit no justification for the use of torture. The regime and its supporters are well aware of the "adverse image" created by the allegations of torture, especially for a regime which bases itself on the motto, "A Greece of Christian Greeks." If a regime uses torture, the ultimate perversion of social relations, to achieve certain ends, these ends, no matter how laudable in theory, risk being perverted. Consequently the Colonels and their defenders abroad have used all the resources at their command to quash the persistent reports of torture.

The Colonels have shown considerable ill-temper over such charges. At a press conference on June 8, 1969, Prime Minister Papadopoulos complained about these "lies" and said that if any proof were given, he would hang those guilty in Constitution Square. Later, on August 2, he told visiting U.S. Congressmen that reports of torture were "so infuriatingly and basely false," that if "evidence of even one such case" were supplied, "then the only duty left to me as a man under solemn military oath is to commit suicide." [*Press Office of the Prime Minister of Greece.* "A Transcription of the August 12, 1969 meeting between Mr. George Papadopoulos, the Prime Minister of Greece, and U.S. Senators and Representatives."] There is perhaps some justification for the Colonels' annoyance, as it is undeniable that in many parts of the world colonels get on with the task of "national regeneration" with hardly a murmur of protest from abroad. Greece, however, is a special case. Though socially and economically it has much in common with underdeveloped countries, it has important institutional and cultural ties with Europe and the West. Greece is a member of NATO, the Council of Europe, and a host of other Western organizations. Modern Greece has enjoyed special attention and affection from philhellenes in particular and Westerners in general who view Greece as the place where "the Western adventure began." To many, rightly or wrongly, barbaric practices are more shocking, simply because they occur in Greece.

The controversy over torture began within a month of the coup. As public debate is not permitted in Greece, the debate was between the new regime and the foreign press and various organizations outside of Greece. The first major article describing methods used in the Athens security police headquarters appeared in *The Guardian* (London) in November, 1967. [This article was written by a British lawyer, Cedric Thornberry. Any investigative reporting on the torture question has been done by visiting journalists. The foreign press corps in Athens, often made up of nationals or those with strong ties to the country, has exercised, as in other totalitarian countries, a self-censorship. Torture is a taboo subject. When Mr. Thornberry tried to enter Greece again in April of 1968 he was refused entry as a "threat to public order."] References to torture then began to appear in the pages of *Le Monde, The Times,* and *The New York Times,* as well as other European and American newspapers. At the end of January, 1968, the London-based humanitarian organization, Amnesty International, released a detailed report based on an investigation made in Greece by two lawyers. [See Documents, Section I, p. 87.] Since Greece is a member of NATO and bound by numerous other agreements to the Atlantic and European communities, the issue was raised in many Western parliaments. Prime Minister Wilson referred in the House of Commons to the "bestialities" committed in Greece. [*The Times,* June 26, 1968.]

Though Great Power politics have determined the current Greek situation, international organizations have played a surprisingly effective role. When the Colonels came to power they no doubt had the notion that the state was absolutely sovereign. However, it must seem to them that every time they turn around some organization which they have never heard of threatens to make an investigation or to expel them. Past Greek governments had routinely attended international conferences and signed innumerable conventions, which now have taken on substance. [Even the NATO preamble has been an embarrassment. "The parties are determined to safeguard the freedom, common heritage and civilization of their peoples founded in the principles of democracy, individual liberty and the rule of law."] Because Greece is a small, strategically located country which depends on international exchange, the Colonels cannot follow their inclination to tell "meddling foreigners" to go to the devil.

The specific issue of torture has made an impression on international organizations: when a trade unionist is tortured the International Labor Organization is upset; when it is a priest, the World Council of Churches reacts; and when it is a military officer, even his former colleagues in NATO begin to wonder. However, the torture issue has been most important in an organization that was designed to protect human rights and to act in precisely this kind of case—the European Commission of Human Rights.

The Commission forms part of the Council of Europe, a regional organization, which brought together the democratic states of Europe after the Second World War. The European Convention of Human Rights, designed to protect the basic civil and political rights of the citizens of a democratic society, was signed in 1950. Article Nineteen created a Commission of Human Rights, which is empowered to hear cases brought by individuals or member states. The basic functions of this Strasbourg-based body are to find the facts of a dispute and try to effect a "friendly settlement." If there can be no "friendly settlement" they report the facts and their recommendations to the Committee of Ministers, made up of the Foreign Ministers of member states, the one body empowered to apply sanctions.

In September of 1967 the governments of Denmark, Norway, Sweden, and the Netherlands filed an application with the Commission charging the Greek government with the violation of most of the basic articles of the Convention. [Applications 3321/67, 3322/67, 3323/67, 3344/67. What makes this case rare in international law is that the complaining states did not bring the action for any direct commercial or territorial gain on behalf of their own nationals. Quite the contrary, they brought it for the principle and application of human rights.] The case dragged on for over a year when the first witnesses were heard in Strasbourg. The human element of human rights engulfed the Commission as they listened to the testimony of torture victims. The Commission held further hearings in December, then went to Greece in March of 1969. They heard more witnesses in Strasbourg in June and July of 1969. Failing to achieve a "friendly settlement" between the parties, the Commission adopted its report on the "Greek Case" on November 5, 1969.

More than half of the twelve hundred pages of this five-volume report deal with the question of torture. The Commission concentrated on sixteen cases, hearing the sixteen victims, as well as forty-two other witnesses, and acted like a court in finding the facts on strict rules of evidence. (The reason for concentrating so thoroughly on a limited number was partly due to time and partly to the refusal of the Greek government to permit twenty-one alleged victims to appear before the Commission in Greece.) The report concludes, "The Commission has found it established beyond doubt that torture or ill-treatment contrary to Article 3 has been inflicted in a number of cases." Most important, they found that torture was a government policy—"an administrative practice."

The Greek government has consistently denied all the charges of torture. The junta has dismissed foreign observers as "part of the international Communist conspiracy" while hostile Greek witnesses have been explained away as "mythomaniacs" or "certified mental cases," or more subtly, those who willingly betrayed their comrades and had to justify their betrayal. While dismissing the sources who claim there is torture, it has presented other sources, most notably the reports of the International Red Cross, which it claims refute the charges. [See Documents, Section II, page 97.] Pressure has been applied on other governments to stifle the issue of torture, in particular the promise of lucrative commercial contracts, which tends to create a tolerant atmosphere. To sway public opinion the regime hired public relations firms outside of Greece to keep pressure on the mass media and governments. [The cost effectiveness of these firms is open to question. The Thomas J. Deegan Co. of New York terminated its contract. Maurice Fraser and Associates of London were involved in a scandal when one of their secret reports to the Greek government revealed that they had a member of Parliament on the payroll. This member of Parliament, Gordon Bagier, had gone on a junket to Greece, and upon his return made public declarations discounting the stories of torture.]

No measures the regime takes to deny the charges of torture can change what has in fact happened and continues to happen. The torture that is practiced today in Greece relies on such techniques as *bastinado* (*falanga*), electroshock, sexual tortures, mock executions, etc. Torture is difficult to define precisely, though easy enough to identify if witnessed or experienced. "Torture" is used in this book in a restricted sense—that is, there must be some systematic physical torture, not just simple beating and not just psychological torture. [Torture is defined here as a systematic and purposive effort over a period of time by a person or persons to compel by means of physical pain and mental anguish a human being to do something he otherwise would not do. Both the Universal Declaration of Human Rights and the European Convention of Human Rights state that "no one shall be subjected to torture" but they do not define it. Article Three of the European Convention is broader in scope: "No one shall be subjected to torture or to inhuman or degrading treatment," a fact of more than academic significance since under Article Fifteen of the Convention a state may suspend certain Articles in time of "grave national emergency" but under no circumstances may it violate Article Three.]

Immediately after the coup the regime arrested thousands of people and beat them up in order to discourage them and others from resisting the new regime. There were some cases of real torture during this period, generally to find out where certain people were hiding, but the phase of systematic torture against those suspected of being engaged in underground activities began in earnest a month after the coup.

The organizations that carry out the torture are the civilian police forces—the security police and the gendarmerie; the armed forces—military police (ESA), army intelligence (A-2), certain elite units such as the marines and LOK, regular units, and the naval intelligence agency; and the state intelligence service, the KYP. [There are two police forces in Greece. One is the city police (*Astinomia*), which is responsible for Athens, Piraeus, Patras, and Corfu. In each *Astinomia* there is a section of the security police (*Asphalia*) who do the torture and have their central headquarters at Bouboulinas Street in Athens. The gendarmerie or rural police (*horofilaki*) are responsible everywhere else in Greece, including a large city like Salonika and many suburbs of Athens. They also have their own *Asphalia* section. Organizations with police functions usually referred to by their initials are: ENA, *Elliniki Nautiki Astinomia,* the Greek navy police; ESA, *Elliniki Stratiotiki Astinomia,* the Greek military police; KYP, *Kratiki Ypiresia Pliroforion,* the state intelligence service; and LOK, *Lochos Orinon Katadromon,* battalion of mountain commandos.] This is the first time in modern Greek peacetime history that the armed forces have arrested, interrogated, and tortured civilians. There is both cooperation and a sense of competition among the different services.

Those who are being tortured today in Greece are those who are suspected of being active in resistance to the military regime. There are certain important qualifications to this statement, as not all men are equal before the torturers. Not all suspects are automatically tortured, but only those who are believed to have useful information and to be susceptible to torture. Though resistance comes from all quarters, the brunt of the regime's brutality has fallen on the Left, both in terms of number tortured and degree of torture. It is generally true, though there are numerous exceptions, that treatment worsens as one moves from right to left on the political spectrum. [This generalization also applies to conditions of imprisonment. The most modern prison in Greece, Koridallos in Piraeus, has individual cells with toilet and shower. There are twenty-four political prisoners there now, twenty-three military officers and one bishop. On the island of Leros there are up to 180 prisoners in one room.] Also the young are worse tortured on the assumption that they can take more. [Of 116 tortured persons whose ages are known, eighty-seven are in the 17–30 age group.] Those known abroad, such as the composer, Mikis Theodorakis, or the sociologist, Vassilis Filias, are generally not physically tortured. (They can also be publicly displayed as proof that there is not torture.)

Why is there torture in Greece today? Though Greece, like other nations, has had no shortage of torture in its long history, there were no known cases of torture of political prisoners since the aftermath of the Civil War. [Demosthenes orated against it, medieval plays described it, the Metaxas dictatorship of the late thirties used it against its political enemies, though not in such a widespread and systematic way as it is used today, and the Greek Civil War precipitated tortures and atrocities on a grand scale. After the fighting stopped, the vengeance of the victors was wreaked on the losers in infamous prison camps. However, since the Karamanlis period of 1955, there has been no known case of torture of political prisoners. Though the practices of the Karamanlis regime toward its political opponents were hardly democratic, torture was not one of them.

The question arises as to whether criminal suspects who did not enjoy the protection of press or political party or wealth were tortured. Here the evidence is not certain, and it is not possible to say without more investigation. The police in Greece have traditionally held the view that a good beating is worth more in crime prevention than the ministrations of any social worker.] The immediate reason why torture is used today in Greece is to gain information about actual or potential resistance and to deter resistance in general. Torture has been effective in its first goal of gaining information and it would appear to have been effective as a deterrent, though it is difficult to judge, not knowing what resistance would have been without the fear of torture. Because the regime cannot count on popular support, there is a definite logic in its use of torture. Torture is employed by those who have seized power to keep power.

Not only are there practical reasons for its use, there are the objective conditions which permit its use. Under martial law any Greek can be arrested anywhere and held incommunicado for any length of time with no obligation on the part of the authorities to give a reason or inform anyone. In contrast to the situation before the coup there is no check on the absolute power of the police and army over the citizen, either through protections which are normally guaranteed by a constitution and enforced by a judiciary or through such means as a press or parliament free to inform the public of government abuses.

To really understand why torture is used today in Greece one must examine the world-view of the military men who made the coup and run Greece. They see the world divided into two species, "the right people" and "the wrong people," as Pattakos has called them, or as Prime Minister Papadopoulos, obsessed with medical imagery, calls them, the "diseased cells" and the "healthy cells." The "right people" are "nationalists," "Christians," and "real Greeks," while the "wrong people" are "communists," "atheists," and "Bulgarians" who want to give away national territory. The "diseased cells" are not really human beings, and human standards cannot be applied to them. This Manicheanism is a common enough phenomenon of human history. In ancient Athens, for example, torture was a heinous crime against a citizen, but against a slave it was perfectly acceptable since a slave was not considered a human being. Problems of conscience for the "righteous" are conveniently resolved if it is believed that those being tortured have forfeited their membership in the human family because of different race, behavior, or ideas. [Racial differences have always been a convenient basis for Manicheanism; expansive peoples have had their "wogs," their "niggers," their "gooks," their "narquis." The state, in identifying itself with the nation, often places its critics outside the pale with "antinational," "antiSoviet," "unAmerican."]

In Greece today this attitude is hardly limited to a few fanatic military officers of little education and with traumatic Civil War experience, but it is shared by "responsible" officers and respectable members of Greek society. This attitude was dramatized for this writer in a dinner conversation in an Athenian home in January of 1968. A pro-junta naval officer, former Commandant of the Navy

Cadets School and now with NATO in Brussels, responded to the subject of torture by saying, "Torture is necessary to defend our civilization." He meant this with all sincerity and no sense of contradiction. It should have been no surprise then that the following month the navy, traditionally the "gentleman's service," was torturing civilians and enlisted men on the laid-up warship, *Elli,* at the Scaramanga Naval Base.

To say that the Greece of 1967 or 1969 is an either-or society of "nationalists" or "communists" is myth. The regime, however, requires this myth to legitimize its power both at home and abroad. They went through the ritual of imprisoning aged people who were labeled "communist" on their police records and had already spent many years in detention; they filled newspapers with stories of communist Civil War atrocities; they made "heroes of the resistance" members of the security battalions who had fought with the Germans against the partisans; in short, they have done their best to resuscitate the hates and fears of the Civil War. However, it was quickly apparent that the two species were only nominally "nationalist" and "communist"; in the real world they were those who were for the Colonels and those who were against them. The junta was the Greek nation. Anybody against the junta was "antinational." "Antinational" means "communist." [*The New York Times Magazine,* September 24, 1967. Pattako is quoted as saying, "In Greece we have right people and wrong people. All those who are against the country are Communists." p. 118.]

The actual situation in Greece does not correspond to the official myth. An omnipotent Communist Party taking orders from the communist monolith in Moscow does not exist, nor did it exist on April 21, 1967. [The Greek Left is currently splintered into numerous factions and small groups. The most important schism is that of the Greek Communist Party (KKE) into two factions (Koliyannis and Partsalides), both claiming legitimacy. This split, latent for many years, was between those of a Stalinist mentality favoring obedience to the Soviet Union, and those of a Titoist bent, favoring a national communism. The coup brought this conflict into the open as the KKE's total lack of preparation exposed the inadequacy of its leadership and policy, just as it exposed on the other side the decadence of the traditional Right. The invasion of Czechoslovakia provided a new issue to exacerbate their internal differences. These groups devote most of their energies to fighting each other. It has come to such a point that there are fistfights in the island detention camps between adherents of the two factions, and relief organizations abroad are handicapped by the fact that they often receive a list of prisoners which includes only those loyal to one of the factions. Aside from the traditional Left, the KKE and the Trotskyites, there are the Maoists, the Guevarists, and the noncommunist socialists who favor a social democratic solution but are also committed to violence as the only way out of the current impasse.] The Soviet Union maintains normal relations with the Colonels and has given the line to its remaining faithful to eschew armed resistance as "adventurism" and concentrate on "mobilizing the masses." The irony is that the real danger of violent overthrow of the regime comes from right-wing military officers, the Center, and non-Moscow left groups. The King, the symbol of anticommunism and traditional values, is in exile. The regime has not only tortured priests and right-wing members of the establishment, but it has arrested, imprisoned, and even tortured fellow military officers. [One of the most striking cases is that of General Koumanakos, the highly praised commander of the Greek contingent in Korea, who was beaten and sent into exile for no apparent reason except that a man of his ability and popularity might prove dangerous in the future. See R. Evans and R. Novak: "Kafka in Greece." *International Herald Tribune,* July 1, 1969.] The reality is so contrary to the picture presented by the junta that even American public opinion, so susceptible to the same two-species view of the universe, has difficulty believing that all those who have unfriendly things to say about the Colonels are really, as Pattakos insists, communists.

A basic issue on the torture question is whether the use of torture is directly ordered by the junta, [After almost three years of this regime, the actual decision-making process is not clearly understood outside the regime. The normal structure of administration with the Ministries and a Prime Minister exists, but there is also a junta of military officers, or two—one large and one small—who operate in complete secrecy and are believed to make the important decisions. The decision to torture would certainly be one of them. The system of government has been compared to the Soviet system, with a Central Committee, a Presidium, and the various Ministries.] or is practiced on an individual and isolated basis by certain army, navy, intelligence, and police personnel. There are certain intermediary possibilities between these two positions. The practice could be not directly ordered but tolerated because the results it produces are considered desirable. Or, for example, there is the position held by the State Department, that "there may well have been individual cases of cruelty and mistreatment," but the authorities have made every effort to prevent them.

The junta is clearly responsible for torture in Greece, not simply in the way government is responsible for the acts of its agents, but because the practice has been known for two and a half years and the regime has taken no known measures to stop it or to punish the guilty. [In fact some defendants have been given up to three years extra for "insulting the tribunal" when they have talked about their tortures at their trials. See *Le Monde,* May 14, 1969, which reports the case of Grigorios Farakos and George Moraitis, each of whom was given three years in addition to their other sentences. The report of the European Human Rights Commission concludes that "the competent Greek authorities, confronted with numerous and substantial complaints and allegations of torture and ill-treatment, have failed to take any effective steps to investigate them or to ensure remedies for any such complaints or allegations found to be true."] Being responsible does not prove that the acts were directly ordered. Only an authentic written order to torture would constitute incontrovertible proof, though it is inherently improbable that this kind of order would ever be written. No written order has been produced abroad, though two persons claim to have seen such orders in Greece. There does exist considerable circumstantial evidence that this is a deliberate practice ordered by the regime.

There are a number of facts that indicate torture is directly ordered from above and is not a matter of individual excess which may or may not be tolerated by the regime. The number of people tortured, which a conservative estimate would place at not less than two thousand, would indicate it is a general practice. Not only is torture widespread, but identical techniques are reported from all over Greece. Prisoners have been tortured by an agency under the jurisdiction of one ministry, then transferred to another and tortured, and in some cases even to an agency of a third Ministry. This implies some central direction. The army, an organization based on obedience to orders given in a hierarchic structure, has been very active in torturing, and it is the army which runs Greece today. The Prime Minister's brother, Col. Costas Papadopoulos, is the *de facto* commander of the notorious military camp, Dionysos, and has daily contact with his brother. The newly formed Marines, which are controlled by Costas and stationed at Dionysos, act as the Prime Minister's Praetorian Guard. Col. Basil Ioannidis, the army's chief torturer, is attached to the office of the army chief of staff, Odysseas Anghelis, and wields considerable power as the spokesman for the "hard line" group of younger officers. Leading members of the junta have made compromising statements [Mr. Pattakos, vice-premier and minister of the interior, told the correspondent of *L'Espresso* in November of 1967 that they beat prisoners in Greece and they should do it in Italy. General Tsevelekos, the Minister of Public Order, said in a speech to men of the gendarmerie in

Salonika on May 11, 1968, "Every kind of violence is occasionally unavoidable and must be used only and solely when the advices, persuasions and warnings have failed to assure the obedience of the people. . . ."] and Col. Yiannis Ladas, the secretary of the ministry of the interior, pistol-whips and beats people in his office. [Signed affidavits by the victims testify to Col. Ladas's behavior. He pistol-whipped and threatened to kill three newspapermen responsible for an article that mentioned homosexuality was practiced in ancient Greece. These three men were J. Lampsas, writer, P. Lambrias, editor, and C. Psychas, the owner of the magazine, *Eikones,* in which the article appeared. The article, "The Third Sex," was in the July 19, 1968, issue. Another affidavit recounts how he whipped a man named George Ladas whom he accused of exploiting his name to better his business.] Rather than investigating allegations of torture, the regime has promoted the torturers and given them letters of commendation. Though their testimony is of doubtful reliability, individual torturers of rank have said to their victims that they were just following orders.

Direct evidence that the junta orders torture derives from the testimony of Constantine Marotis, the only person to get out of Greece who has taken part in high-level security operations. Marotis was a promising young naval officer who came from a traditionally military family. He enjoyed top NATO security clearance and was made a security officer after the coup. He remained loyal to the king, however, and six day's after Constantine's abortive counter-coup, Lieutenant Commander Marotis left Greece.

Marotis sat on the "Coordination Council for Information of Piraeus," which was set up by the junta to supervise security operations in the Piraeus and South Aegean area. It was run by the military and brought together security officers from both civilian and military organizations. [The Council was made up of Col. Kourtis, Military Governor of Piraeus, Chairman of the Council; Capt. Petmezas, Royal Hellenic Navy, Vice-Chairman; Mr. Tsiougas, Chief of Police of Piraeus; Mr. Gianakopoulos, Chief of the Piraeus *Asphalia;* Mr. Kouvas, Vice-Director of the Piraeus *Asphalia;* Major Karatsoyiannis commanding officer of the KYP in Piraeus; Col. Komninos, Chief of the gendarmerie for Piraeus and the Central Aegean. Other members included the harbor master of Piraeus, a Merchant Marine Captain, and all the security officers assigned to the above-named officers.] The Council appears to have enjoyed an absolute power over the people and property of the area. In Council meetings Marotis reports that torture was openly discussed, and they had orders from Pattakos to shoot certain people in hiding when they were found. Marotis joined in one massive manhunt and in two days came across three other bodies washed up on shore, dead by violent means. Torture methods were demonstrated to him by a KYP major, and he saw a prisoner being tortured in the Piraeus Security Police Headquarters. He also says that in his capacity as security officer of a base he received from General Anghelis a top secret circular order which stated that care should be taken while torturing so that no marks would be left.

One day Marotis received an order to deliver a prisoner named Bashari Karaosman to a top-secret camp outside of Athens. The existence of this camp raises certain unanswered questions about foreign involvement. To explore these questions it is necessary to review the role of the United States in Greece and examine in particular the role of the KYP and the American C.I.A.

Greece, situated between East and West, has in its long history felt the dominion of most of the great empires. In 1821 Greeks fought a war of independence against the Ottoman Turks, yet they were never to achieve real independence, for their destiny was to be decided in the chancelleries of the Great Powers, most notably England. In 1947, during the Greek Civil War, the British were no longer able to support the burdens of empire, and they abruptly announced to Washington that they were pulling out of Greece. President Truman, in what was to prove a momentous decision, decided to replace England as Greece's primary source of economic and military aid. On March 12, 1947, President Truman, speaking to a special joint session of Congress, said, "I believe that it must be the policy of the United States to support free peoples who are resisting attempted subjugation by armed minorities or by outside pressures." This became known as the "Truman Doctrine." Twenty years later America would find itself with an empire and Greece would find itself with a military dictatorship. The Greeks, a free people, would be subjugated by a minority armed by the United States, and the outside pressures would be American.

Greece was the first country of the Old World to experience the full impact of *Pax Americana*. Aid and advisors of every kind arrived: agronomists, soldiers, teachers, spies, businessmen, diplomats. Economically Greece was integrated into the Western system; militarily, the Greek armed forces were equipped, trained, and supervised by the U.S.; and politically, Greece was a satellite of the U.S. in the bipolar world of the cold war. Many Greeks, accustomed in a small country to a limited independence, welcomed the United States in the years when they were fighting a bitter Civil War and feared Slavic expansion. Greece was a loyal ally for the United States.

KYP was founded in 1953 under the government of Field Marshall Papagos. Though there was an army intelligence service (A-2), it was felt that a new central intelligence agency was needed for modern times. KYP was modelled after and remains to this day largely financed by the American C.I.A. It is, in fact, though not in law, a subsidiary of the Langely, Virginia, parent corporation. Under the laws that created it, KYP was to concern itself with counter-espionage activities outside of Greece. It was not to interfere in any way with Greek domestic affairs, and it was to be directly responsible to the Prime Minister. From the very first, however, KYP and the American C.I.A. became heavily involved in Greek internal affairs.

In Greece KYP kept a regular tap on important telephones, including those of government Ministers, became involved in army plots, and generally enjoyed an autonomy and power that provided immunity from criticism. When George Papandreou came to power in 1964 there was a head-on clash when he tried to bring the organization to heel. KYP resisted these attempts and in the process tasted their first public criticism in the Greek press when the new government revealed that KYP's financial support came directly from the C.I.A. without passing through any Greek ministry.

Part of the heavy involvement of KYP and the C.I.A. in domestic Greek affairs can be explained by their concept of the enemy. The enemy was not simply expansionist Russia but communism. There were Greeks who were communists and took orders from Moscow, and thus foreign subversion could come from one's own compatriots. Therefore KYP and the C.I.A. were active in keeping track of the political beliefs and activities of Greek citizens. Both the C.I.A. and KYP, living in a two-species world, saw as "communist" any criticism either of established institutions or of their actions.

KYP plays an important role in the Greece of the Colonels. Directors of KYP have always been army men, and KYP maintains close relations with the army. Its current chief, General Hadzipetro, is a member of the inner junta, and his agents are very important both in Greece and abroad. Given that Papadopoulos and the junta leaders have been members of this intelligence community, [The head of the C.I.A. in Greece, Mr. James M. Potts, is fond of boasting in Athenian circles that Prime Minister Papadopoulos is "his son."] it can be argued that Greece is a nation where a modern intelligence establishment has captured state power. The standards of their secret and amoral world have become the standards of government.

In the 1950's the Balkans were an important cold war arena for the various intelligence services. The C.I.A. maintained a large staff in Greece, enlisting many Greek-Americans. Its activities directed outside the country ranged from the overt, such as monitoring radio broadcasts, to the covert, such as dropping over a hundred men into Albania to overthrow the regime. The C.I.A. group which was in charge of the Bulgarian operation was based in Kavala, a seaport and tobacco center in the north of Greece. They operated under the cover of the U.S.I.S. and the American Agricultural Mission. One of their standard methods for gathering intelligence was to interrogate Bulgarians who had either escaped or been kidnapped by their agents. Their activity became something of a scandal in Kavala, and they moved out of town to the estate of a wealthy American tobacco merchant named Turner, who was married to a Greek. This house was on the sea and relatively isolated. The local people say that this place was used for interrogation and that at least one Bulgarian died under torture there. In fairness to the American C.I.A., it must be pointed out that the actual "interrogation" was done by their Greek colleagues and it appears that the Americans made an effort to restrain them in their propensity to use those brutal methods that have characterized relations with their Balkan neighbors for centuries.

In 1957 the C.I.A. set up a camp outside of Athens at a place called Aghia Paraskevi, which is below Mount Hymettos. This camp was used to interrogate people coming from the Iron Curtain countries. It appears that in the first years there was cooperation with other NATO countries, and their intelligence services used the facilities when a prisoner or refugee had information of particular value to the country concerned. Before the coup this camp was top secret.

Though reports of a camp in that area began to filter out of Greece after the coup, the first specific details came from Lieutenant Commander Marotis, who had delivered the prisoner Karaosman there. Marotis said that the man who presented himself as the commander of the camp, Lieutenant Colonel Zourelis, of KYP, showed him the camp and its equipment. The KYP man told the naval officer, "Don't worry, we will get the truth here because we have all the scientific methods." Marotis described the camp as being in a pine grove next to a Marine camp. There are eight soundproof bungalows inside a fenced-off area, staffed by both civilian and military personnel. Doctors are there to provide a medical control to the interrogation methods, especially the use of "truth drugs." Zourelis lost his right forearm and eye in the Middle East during World War II. He wears a plastic prosthesis covered by leather with which, witnesses say, he enjoys beating those fortunate to have two hands. He told the sub-Commission in Greece that he was unable to use his arm, but he refused to have a medical examination to determine this.

When Marotis went back days later to pick up the prisoner, Karaosman was a human wreck. There were not only marks of injections on his left arm, but his back was covered with "stripes of blood". The sailor told Marotis about his tortures, saying they were so bad he had tried to hang himself with his shirt.

Marotis referred to the Aghia Paraskevi as a "NATO camp," which prompted questions from the floor of European parliaments that were never satisfactorily answered. Spokesmen for the Greek regime told the Human Rights Commission in Strasbourg that the Aghia Paraskevi Aliens Interrogation Center, which had been built with "allied funds," was exclusively for the debriefing of Iron Curtain refugees, and it was done in cooperation with "NATO headquarters." They said that the camp worked in Cooperation with the World Council of Churches and the United Nations High Commission for Refugees. The World Council gave "financial help" and the High Commission had a representative at the camp to help place refugees. The World Council of Churches and the High Commissioner wrote the Human Rights Commission that they had never heard of this camp, much less financed it or cooperated in its operation.

It is not clear what role, if any, the C.I.A. now plays at Aghia Paraskevi. There is no direct evidence as to whether or not they are still involved in the camp's administration. There is direct evidence that the KYP which has been financed by the C.I.A., has tortured at least one Greek there. Karaosman said that he was beaten with a "thick white double cable." Descriptions of this particular torture instrument have come from other torture centers in Greece. At the Bouboulinas St. *Asphalia* headquarters, the torturers have told prisoners that this special white whip comes as U.S. aid, and is "scientific," making their work easier. According to a former prisoner, the *Asphalia* told him that the military police received as American military aid headscrews ("iron wreaths"), and the military police had refused to give any of their allotment to the civilian police, much to the annoyance of the latter. Evidence based on the statements of the torturers who lied under oath before the European Commission is hardly the most reliable, but at the very least there are questions raised that should be answered. It might be one thing for the C.I.A. to train and equip Greeks to torture foreign agents, a nasty necessity in the defense of "freedom," but it is another to finance and aid the torture of Greeks and the suppression of their freedom.

This is only part of the larger question, and that is that the

United States government is the principle support for a military regime, a member of NATO, which violates every basic human right and depends on widespread torture to stay in power. Though many Greeks believe that the United States, through the C.I.A., was behind the coup of April 21, 1967, there has never been sufficient evidence presented to prove this charge. A more likely candidate is the Pentagon, which through its liaison officers of the American Military Mission in Greece, was at least aware of the preparations. The Pentagon has in fact been the strongest supporter of the Colonels, both in Greece and in Washington. Whether or not an agency of the U.S. government planned and executed the coup to avoid the election of the liberal George Papandreou remains only conjecture, and, though interesting, is not particularly relevant. What is relevant is the policy of the United States toward the coup. The United States has supported the Colonels from the outset and has behaved as though the junta were a "solution." The U.S. has given money, arms, and diplomatic support to keep this regime in power, justifying it on the grounds, not unlike those the Russians have cited in Czechoslovakia, that the interests of the NATO alliance demand it and the situation in the Mediterranean and Middle East is so precarious that secure bases in Greece are more important than democracy in Greece.

If American support is obvious to the Greeks, it is vital to the torturers. The torturers themselves not only use American equipment in their military and police work, but they rely on the fact that the U.S. supports them. Hundreds of prisoners have listened to the little speech given by Inspector Basil Lambrou, who sits behind his desk which displays the red, white, and blue clasped-hand symbol of American aid. He tries to show the prisoner the absolute futility of resistance: "You make yourself ridiculous by thinking you can do anything. The world is divided in two. There are the communists on that side and on this side the free world. The Russians and the Americans, no one else. What are we? Americans. Behind me there is the government, behind the government is NATO, behind NATO is the U.S. You can't fight us, we are Americans."

CASE HISTORIES

The following are the stories, in their own words, of ten Greeks who have been tortured. The cases have been selected from the available affidavits with the intention of presenting people of diverse social background and political views who come from different areas of Greece. These cases are fairly typical; they do not represent extreme examples. Some of the individuals presented here have not been badly tortured but are of special interest for other reasons.

These documents have all been signed by the victims. Some of those who tell their stories have escaped from Greece, while others are in the relative security of prison. All have given their express permission that their stories be published in this book. Those who have managed to escape abroad all strongly emphasize that their story is just one story out of hundreds, and they who, by chance, have escaped are speaking not for themselves alone but for all those anonymous people in Greece who have shared the same experience.

Each case is introduced by a note giving the background of the person. The information for these notes was provided by personal interviews when possible or by documents and friends of the victims when interviews were not possible. Unless otherwise stated, these accounts have been translated from the Greek originals.

KATERINA ARSENI—Actress

"Kitti" Arseni was born on the island of Cephalonia in 1936. She had a happy childhood in a close-knit family, enjoying the free and untroubled life of the relatively well-to-do on a poor but beautiful island. When she was thirteen, her father, a bank manager, moved the family to Athens. He died very shortly after that, and her mother, two brothers, and Kitti were suddenly without means of support. It was a struggle; the four of them lived in two rooms. Kitti graduated at seventeen from a strict girls' school in Athens with her mind made up to become an actress. But for three years she had to work at various jobs to help support the family.

When she was twenty she entered the best drama school in Athens, the Theater Art School, run by the leading personality of the Athenian theater, Koun. Though she continued to work mornings and went to classes in the afternoon, these were wonderful stagestruck years of absolute absorption in the theater. She was offered a job by Koun when she finished her studies, but chose to start a repertory theater with some of her classmates. They travelled around Greece playing to good reviews and empty houses. After a year they gave up their experiment.

She took parts as they came along, but she was restless and dissatisfied with the superficial plays that were standard fare. Acting was more than having your picture in the newspapers. In 1964 she worked in a kibbutz in Israel, and in 1965 she toured around Western Europe and realized more than ever how much there was to do in Greece. The sixties were a time of great ferment and change in Greece, not only in politics but also in all the arts. With the murder of Lambrakis by the Right in 1963 and the King's "coup" in 1965, more and more theater people took active political positions. Kitti's generation, in questioning the established theater, were also led to question the role of theater in society and to question the society itself. Kitti became more active politically, but joined no party. The *Asphalia* was furious that they could find no file on her when they arrested her.

Before the coup she was planning with friends to open a theater in a suburb of Athens where they could have real contact with the audience and perform *engagé* plays. The night of the coup she was playing in Salonika. When she got the news she rushed back to

Athens. "I had the feeling that suddenly I was in the middle of a battle. There was a war so now we have to fight." The daily life of the theater was no longer important, what was important was to be "free." The question of whether or not to get involved never entered her mind; soon she was engaged in trying to organize resistance and distribute tracts. They were inexperienced and too enthusiastic, perhaps, for clandestine work, but that summer there was a great sense of solidarity among all kinds of people who were working together for a common cause.

The following affidavit was written in English.

I was arrested on August 23, 1967. Three plainsclothesmen belonging to the Athens Security Police entered my house at two o'clock at night. The first one to enter introduced himself: "I am Lambrou." I later learned that the names of the other two were Mallios and Babalis. Lambrou, Mallios and Babalis were to become my regular interrogators. Under the surveillance of Lambrou I was restricted to one roof of my house while the other two embarked upon a detailed search of the house (they turned drawers upside down, opened trunks, etc.). My mother suffers from a heart condition; while the search was on, she suffered a light heart attack.

When the search was over, Mallios and Babalis came to the room where I was isolated. They had found three mimeographed leaflets printed by an underground resistance group, the Patriotic Front, several books "forbidden" by the junta and some records with music written by Theodorakis. All three started interrogating me and questioned me about the leaflets and about a tape containing a message by Theodorakis which, according to their information, was passed on to me for delivery abroad. They wanted the names of my collaborators and the tape. While questioning me, they pulled my hair and Babalis drew his revolver and threatened to kill me. Since I was terribly worried about my mother's condition, and since I was told that I was under arrest anyway, I asked them to leave the house. They broke the records by Theodorakis, took away any book which appeared to them to be "leftish" and then asked me to take a blanket with me and we left the house.

At the entrance to the building the driver of the car was waiting. He brought the car from the street corner to the entrance. In the back seat I sat between Mallios and Babalis while Lambrou sat in the front. The car moved.

Because I refused to answer their questions, Lambrou ordered the driver to drive to "Damaria" (a deserted quarry in Athens). The car turned on Galatsiou Street which leads to "Tourkovounia." They started beating me hard on the head—I believe with the edge of their palms. They threatened that in "Damaria" they would strip me and execute me unless I spoke. The car stopped at a relatively deserted area and they began twisting my wrists and fingers and threatening to break bones. The pain was excruciating. Seeing a light in the distance, I screamed as hard as I could. Then the car moved ahead again and we reached a totally deserted area. They made me lie on the back seat and left the two rear doors open. Mallios lay over me, holding me firmly, and shut my mouth with his hand. I saw the driver holding two long truncheons made of either rubber or twisted and pliable wood. Somebody took off my shoes and I believe the driver started hitting hard on the soles of my feet (*falanga*). The pain on the soles of my feet was very intense. After a while they stopped and made me walk barefooted on the stones and thorns, beating me on all parts of my body and head as I walked. I was bleeding from my mouth and my nose. Finally they stopped. Babalis took out his gun and placed it against my temple; he threatened to execute me if I didn't give them the information they wanted. At that moment my psychological situation was such that death seemed a salvation and I did not react at all. This infuriated them more, and they began to beat me again and to curse at me. I don't know how much time passed as I was groggy when Lambrou ordered them to stop and to take me to the Security Police Headquarters and to pass me through the "machine of truth." (As I later learned, there is a machine in the Security Police and in Military Hospital 401: *"Electric Shock."*)

In the Security Police on Bouboulinas Street I was booked and handed over to the regular duty officer. The office clock showed that it was 5:30 A.M. He took me down to the basement, to the "inner isolation block," cell number 18.

The cells in the isolation block measure approximately one meter fifty (1,50) by one meter eighty (1,80). The floor was broken, uneven cement, completely bare, without furnishings, bed, chair, etc., full of "punaise" and very dirty. The waste from the WC outside, which often overflowed, filled the cell. There is almost no air or light. I lay down on the dirty, damp, cement with only my thin summer dress separating my body from the floor. For the first days I had food which my mother had brought. (The detainees who had no relatives had to buy the evening and afternoon meal from the security police canteen for twenty-five drachmas a day. If they had neither relatives nor money, they went hungry.) They often called me for many hours of exhausting interrogations, especially in the evening and after midnight. My main interrogators were Lambrou, Babalis and Mallios although there were also others who changed often because of their own fatigue. (Some of the others are Yannicopoulos, Kolonias and Yanakakos.) The pressure and, the tactics used are varied. Blackmail, threats of reprisals to my family, fear of my future and my life, bribery, offers of money and promises of better treatment.

The fifth day after my arrest Lambrou ordered, "strict isolation." This means that the detainee does not go out of his cell *even to use the WC.* He is obliged to urinate and defecate in his cell. *He is given neither food nor water. I* remained thus for four days. I was only taken out for interrogation during this time. I lost a great deal of weight, was continuously dizzy, and my head still hurt from the previous beatings. After four days of the "strict isolation" I returned to "regular isolation." I then had a blanket and my family brought food every day. Forbidden items were: soap, toothpaste, towels, comb and brush, etc. Conversation too is forbidden. The guard would hit you if he heard you talking, singing or whistling. Visiting relatives and lawyers, any kind of message or letter and medicine are also forbidden.

On the eleventh day they moved me to cell number 12 where I was put together with another woman, hysterical and ill—also a political detainee. We couldn't lie down, we sat only with our knees up, the lack of air was choking us, making us delirious and senseless. Instead of falling asleep we would fall into a coma. I stayed in cell number 12 under these conditions for nine days. On the twentieth day they moved me to cell number 14. On the same evening they again took me for interrogation and handed me over to an interrogator named Spanos, completely dry of emotion, cold-blooded, faceless, expressionless, with his three assistants. (Of the three others, I remember one young blond with bulging muscles in his arms, another very short and thin man; of the third I remember nothing.) They led me to the "taratsa." This is a room on the terrace like an old washing shed. It has two or three showers on the left side as you enter. Near these showers there must be a machine which makes the noise resembling the motor of a motor-cycle to cover the screaming. This room is about 2.50 by 3.50 meters, one thick bench in the middle with rope and to the right of the bench a large cauldron which they also hit with iron to make a loud gong to cover the screams. This description may be a little confused because of my psychological state and secondly because it was almost completely dark. I yelled to them that I wanted to see, but Spanos, the "commander-in-chief," wanted to work on me according to his own system of psychological pressures and stopped one of his men who had moved to turn on the light. They left only the door open and there was some natural light. They lay me down on the bench and tied me tightly from my feet to my shoulders. One of them began to beat me in the *falanga* style. They ripped my clothing off, exposing my shoulder, stepped on my stomach, held my throat tightly as if to strangle me, and lit matches near my eyes. Spanos gave instructions to the torturers, ordering them when to continue and when to stop. He continuously asked me for names, he pulled my hair and beat my head against the bench. The cauldron was gonged to cover my screams after the motorcycle machine was already on. When I shouted a great deal, they stuffed my mouth with a rag, to cover the screaming still more and to cause a feeling of suffocation. In the meantime the *falanga* continued. Since I had the past experience of being beaten at "Damaria" on the night of my arrest, I would like to say this: although the pain was almost unbearable, the basic feeling was not pain but fear. I had the impression that I was surrounded by insane and twisted men who, on the one hand knew how to carry out their work scientifically (where and how much to beat, how to frighten a person who has been placed in their hands, how to paralyze the physical resistance the body may be able to muster, without leaving any marks), and on the other hand, their "working hours" were the ones of pleasure and sexual gratification. They threatened me with death, saying that they would throw me from the terrace to the street, through a hole to the basement. But even this is something which you almost wish would happen. I don't know how many hours had passed. I was half-conscious when they untied me. I could not walk. They carried me to an office on the fourth floor and they tried to revive me. They gave me water, looked at my feet to see if anything was broken, someone checked my pulse, perhaps Dr. Kyoupis. I was suffering from nervous shock, unable to speak and continuously shaking. I came to after a long time. Then they came. (The interrogators Lambrou, Mallios, Babalis.) They began to interrogate me again for some hours. They threatened me with the machine again and by saying, "You will see what will happen to you; this was nothing, don't think that we are finished." Finally they ordered me to go down to my cell and told me in an official tone that they would achieve their purpose by using any means necessary, refusing all responsibility for my fate.

They did not bring me to the "taratsa" again. Perhaps even they had the same fear of my condition. I couldn't stand on my feet. I was very weak and I couldn't sleep at all waiting for the hour when they would call me again. I fell into a coma. The interrogations and the blackmail continued for days. Psychological pressure became even greater. They frightened me with innumerable reprisals against my family which I well knew they could carry out. They gathered evidence against me and succeeded in extracting information about my activities with force and inhuman means and drew up my accusation, putting me, as they did all the others, under law 509/1947. Even though there was a formal announcement common to this accusation, and my file was closed on the thirtieth day after my arrest, I nevertheless spent eight additional days in solitary confinement. During this period they called me for interrogation many times just to see if they could force more information out of me to help their case.

One day they suddenly brought my brother to me. He was without belt and without a cap, which means that a soldier is in prison. He was between two army officers. They threatened at the same time my brother and me. They told my brother that he had responsibility for me because we lived in the same house. Lambrou told me that because of me my brother has suffered many things. My duty was to save my brother. They said to him: "If you are an honest soldier, you have to interrogate her." They wanted my brother to hit me.

On the thirty-ninth day, they took me from solitary confinement to the fourth floor to a room-type cell with seven other girls. I had a mouth infection, swollen gums; I wasn't

able to chew; my teeth hurt because of this infection and I
suffered from very bad headaches. Before my arrest I had
had an operation on my ear and thus my hearing was
impaired because of my treatment in Security Police Headquarters. I don't think it necessary to explain my psychological condition.

Even though the isolation cells were completely sealed,
and the little iron window could be opened only by the
guard, I still knew approximately what was going on and
who else was suffering simultaneously during my thirty-
eight days in solitary. Some hole in the broken floor of the
cell, a careless action of the guard when he opened the
door for me to go to the WC or for interrogation, helped
me to conclude that I had a relatively light treatment in
detention. I saw men walking on their elbows and knees,
crawling on their stomachs, perhaps with broken ribs, damaged spines, feet completely split open and broken, heads
and faces maimed, misshapen. The majority of men were
not able to walk. The treatment of the men is more severe
than that of the women. The beatings on the head and on
the stomach provoke serious circumstances, with hemor-
rhages from the chest and stomach. Once the situation of a
detainee was so serious that they had to rush him out of
his isolation, probably taking him to 401 military hospital.
I also know many cases in which even though they were
taken to 401 in a critical and dangerous condition, once
there they were given electric shock.

In some cases where it was *necessary* to extract a "confession" or information by force, the torturers were extremely hard and the presence of Dr. Kyoupis was necessary. He takes the pulse and tells if it is possible or not
to continue the beating. I know of a case of torture where
the man being tortured asked for water and was given
chlorine. In ESA (Military Police) the detainees were left
hanging by their shoulders, hands behind their backs, for
hours. They hold out the tongue with pliers and burn the
body with matches and cigarettes.

The electric shock takes place in the Security Police
and in 401. In hospital 401 they are taken after already
having been beaten. The "doctors" tell them when they
show their wounds that they are "insane" and that electric
shock must be applied. There are cases of detainees who
after arriving in a state of coma to 401, undergo electric

shock continuously for one week. The following week it was
no longer necessary to touch the wires to the body because
the body was so conditioned that the mere suggestion of
electric shock would produce the spasm. This was done
surrounded by laughing "doctors."

Women have suffered sexual tortures, especially the young
students. This kind of torture is applied by a special student
section ("spouthastiko") of the security police headed by
Karapanayiotis and Gravaritis. A woman pregnant three
months miscarried in solitary after having been beaten.
She was taken for two days to Alexandra hospital and
afterwards was again put in solitary confinement where she
remained for forty days. The men were often tortured by
twisting and beating of the genital organs which provoke
serious complications.

When I was in solitary, a man went crazy; the detainee
in cell number 16 woke early one morning at four A.M.
and started beating his head against the wall, screaming
for help and pleading with them to stop beating him and not
to execute him. Two guards took him down, handcuffed
him and tied him up inside his cell. Thus he remained for
about four days. He often suffered hallucinations, thinking
that they were beating his mother and raping his sister in
front of him, executing his brother in the army. I don't
know if they gave him a sedative or offered him any
medical attention. I do know that each time he began to
shout, the guards would let him shout for a while and let
him cause self-inflicted wounds for some time, and finally
they would begin to hit him themselves. This case provoked
panic in the other cells continuously. The guards' watch
became stronger. They began beating everyone, especially
the detainees in the corridor. (Because of the number of
arrests which were continuous throughout this period, the
cells were overcrowded. There was a problem of space.)
The corridors were narrow, no more than half a meter
wide. Many detainees stayed in the corridors filled with the
dirt and water from the WC without moving throughout the
day and night. In the most overcrowded times, they remained seated and it was forbidden to turn to the right or
left to the other detainees. In front of me, a guard named
Panayiotis, about two meters tall, beat a sixteen- or seven-
teen-year-old boy so much that it made him hemorrhage
from the mouth. The atmosphere is so nightmarish every-

where, in solitary, in the big common cells (the "Pigada"), in the interrogation offices, on the fourth floor, that attempted suicides by both men and women were numerous.

Anything that I have said about other people, those other than myself, *is absolutely true, but I refuse to give any names, knowing that these men are still in danger, wherever they are, in prison, in exile or in their homes.*

I was a detainee on the fourth floor for twenty-one days waiting for the papers to transfer me to the prison. Life there was rather normal. There is light, you know if it is day or night, there is bedding, water for washing, paper and pencil, books (subject to censorship), ten-minute visits of relatives twice a week, but no lawyer was permitted. There I underwent another type of torture. The room-type cell which faced an interior courtyard was exactly across from the "taratza." During all the days and nights, more often the nights, we heard the noise of the motorcycle machine, the noise of the cauldron, cries and screams of those being tortured. I still retain the awful memory of this torture. To answer those who feel that it is impossible for torture to exist at the security police on Bouboulinas Street and especially on the "taratza" where the other houses are so close, I assure them, *it does exist and they can hear it.* There are days during the visiting hours when we can hear the screaming and we try and hide it from our relatives so they don't become crazy with worry. The sounds during the night are like nightmares. We often had hysterical crises, even among the girls with the strongest nerves.

After sixty-two days of being kept in the security police, I was taken to the women's prison in Averoff. I was tried in the Patriotic Front trial of thirty-one from the fifteenth to the twenty-first of November, 1967, under law 509/1947 and with a special personal accusation: distribution of illegal printed material and sending a tape abroad with a message by Mikis Theodorakis. I was sentenced to three years in a prison and the sentence was suspended.

During my stay in the security police, in prison and in meetings after my release with people who had been through the places of torture—Security Police, ESA, 401 Military Hospital, the military camp of Dionysos, Security Police of Thessalonika and the security police of other towns in Greece, I am able to know and to accuse for the benefit of those organizations which fight for basic human rights and for the benefit of the general public that *in the military regime now ruling Greece, tortures take place officially sanctioned and scientifically organized for the purposes of extracting information and doing away with any physical or moral resistance on the part of the individual and to destroy his individual personality. Those men, regardless of political beliefs, as long as these beliefs are deemed "suspicious" by the Colonels, are in danger of an immediate attempt to break them down both psychologically and physically.*

At the Patriotic Front trial in November Kitti received a three-year suspended sentence. She went home to her mother, who had been desperately upset. The *Asphalia* had failed to break her, failed to get any information, but Kitti was a physical and nervous wreck. Whenever she did manage to go to sleep, she woke up terrorized by her nightmares of broken images of the *Asphalia*. In the spring of 1968 she succeeded in leaving Greece "illegally." As her brother was still in the army, she was unable to speak. He was discharged in October and managed to leave the country. Kitti Arseni was the first torture victim to speak before the European Human Rights Commission in Strasbourg at the end of November, 1968. Her testimony had great impact.

Today she is an exile. She lives in the splintered left milieu of the Paris Greeks. Now she sleeps better. But in her quick gestures and in her eyes there is still the experience of Bouboulinas Street. For a long time she has not gone to the theater, thinking somehow it would be a betrayal to those Greeks back in Greece, those who are still in prison, those now suffering in the *Asphalia*. But she is a woman of artistic temperament: "I have the need to express myself, it is there." Now after two years, she is ready to work again.

PETROS GAVALAS—Priest

The case of Petros Gavalas, a village priest from Crete, is not one of barbaric tortures, compared with hundreds of other cases. The method applied to him is the simple and "humane" one used by South Africans and the British on Cyprus. The prisoner is simply made to stand in one place for hour after hour. The deposition of Father Petros is of interest as it is so profoundly Greek. Anyone who has read the last novel of Nikos Kazantsakis, *The Fratricides,* will quickly recognize that the hero of the novel, Father Yiannaros, and Father Petros are kindred spirits. Both share a love for Greece and God, and when confronted with cruelty they both choose to act. Petros Gavalas comes from a tradition of Orthodox priests who historically have felt it their duty not to fold their hands before foreign oppression and domestic tyranny, but to resist.

STATEMENT of Petros Gavalas, Priest, resident of Aghios
Thomas, Monofatsion, Heraklion, Crete.

Whereas God is omniscient and omnipotent He could have made human beings incapable of doing evil, in which case men would be simply machines or animals guided by instinct;

Whereas on the contrary, He created man in His own image, that is He endowed man with mind and free will;

Whereas also the Lord Jesus Christ, who took human form for the sake of man, being also perfect God, consubstantial with the Father and the Holy Spirit, could have said, "Everybody must believe in me" what He in fact said was, "Let anyone who chooses me, follow me."

Whereas our Greek national history is full of the wisest lessons and sayings of our forefathers concerning the human condition and human rights, such as, for example, "Happiness is Freedom" of Thucydides, etc.;

Whereas totalitarian regimes and social systems under any color, red or black, and under any name, communism or fascism, abolish precisely the mind and free will of man and reduce individuals and peoples to the state of animals;

Whereas all intellectuals, scientists, and especially religious officials, like the under-signed, have a duty to fight for the human personality and for the blessings of freedom and democracy;

Whereas on the twenty-first of April, 1967, a dictatorship of the harshest kind was imposed on the Greek people by a coup d'etat, without sufficient or necessary reason, and whereas the de-humanization of the Greek people was boldly undertaken,

For the above reasons,

I hold it to be my duty to fight with all my powers against this harsh dictatorship which has been imposed on my beloved country until our Christian and civilized people regain their freedom and their human rights, but always by spiritual and intellectual means, means which would never be inconsistent with my religious capacity.

I acted on this decision from the beginning of May, 1967, when I was convinced of the real intentions of the so-called "revolution," by advising, preaching, encouraging and appropriately enlightening the people. Consequently I took part in the Pan Cretan meeting held in Aghiasma, Milopotamou, Rethimnis, Crete, of which I had the honor of being chairman and which took place on October 28, 1967.

I was arrested by the police on the night of the 9th–10th November, 1967. I was taken to the Gendarmerie of Heraklion, where I had to appear in my pyjamas before an officer named Kanypasis who asked me in a severe tone, "Priest, did you bless those people, did you bless them with Holy Water?" I did not reply. After a while, he demanded that I talk. When I refused to give the names of certain persons and when I was unable to tell things about which I really did not know, he started to beat me. He ordered his men to handcuff me and they took me and threw me in a closed van. I later was led into a dark room where they ordered me to stand at attention facing the wall.

I remained in this position for about thirty hours and when I asked them to free my hands so that I could urinate, they refused. (These were men whom I did not know, they were dressed in civilian clothes.) As a result I had to urinate in my clothes three times. When, finally, I was too tired to stand up, I sank to my knees. My guard ordered me to get up, but since I could not carry out his order, immediately he pushed me and I fell on the floor. He then, either deliberately or not, stepped on my left foot, opening a slight wound. I still was not able to get up so he grabbed me by the hair and shook me so violently that many of my hairs remained in his hand, while I, full of sorrow, turned my eyes to him looking for sympathy and compassion and received instead a most vulgar insult. At the same time he took my head and banged it against the wall, but I lost consciousness. When I came to later on, my left eardrum had been damaged and was bleeding. Twenty-seven days later I was transferred from the dungeons of Heraklion and Chania Security Service to the reform prison of Chania. There I asked for a doctor who was a specialist, but only the prison doctor gave me medicine, and this was obviously not appropriate because pus continued to come out of my ear for seven months. It was only after my transfer to Heraklion that I was cured after an ear specialist saw me.

From the above police officers I was able to find out the name of Sergeant Trochalakis who directed at me the most horrible insults, as for example, "You are only worth spitting on, you inprincipled satan, crook, coward, dog, etc., and if you had a conscience you would immediately unfrock yourself." A certain policeman, Choulakis, was continually threatening me with bodily harm, saying things like, "I will make you vomit up everything you know, you dog, etc. Don't try and play the brave one with me . . . I'm going to pull out your beard, hair by hair, and take out your teeth one by one. I'll stomp on your stomach so your intestines will come out your mouth." Such unfortunately has been the attitude of officers and regular Greek policemen, compatriots of mine, towards a priest, that is towards me, who had dedicated all his efforts to the service of the church and nation.

What can I say about the twenty-seven days that I was kept in dank and dark unsanitary cells? Throughout this time, they never allowed any relative, not even my unhappy wife, to come to see me and bring me some clothes so I would be able to keep warm. (It was November and December.) We were not given proper food and only those with money could order something to eat. Ever since I have been suffering from laryngitis, and still my vocal cords do not work properly. I have lost my voice and perhaps I will never be able to fulfill my religious duties. That is, if they ever appoint me again, which I fear they will not do.

In finishing this statement of mine, I would like to ask the European Commission of Human Rights, the governments of the civilized world and its religious leaders to sympathize with Greece and the unhappy Greek people and to help them by word and deed to get rid of their calamity.

Furthermore, I ask all the philanthropic organizations of the world to give financial help to the suffering families of political prisoners, many of whom are in dire need, including the undersigned,

Petros Gavalas

Aghios Thomas
March 17, 1969

Petros Gavalas was released from prison before the European Human Rights Commission visited Athens in March of 1969. The priest had been named as a witness and had received an official summons. Despite threats, he and his wife, the *papadia,* went to Athens. In the meantime, however, the sub-Commission had decided not to examine any witnesses who were related to the Marketakis affair, as they had refused to examine Marketakis again. [See page 39 for full details of the "Marketakis Affair."] Since Gavalas was a prisoner at the same time in Crete as Marketakis, they decided not to hear him. Gavalas, however, armed with his summons, went to the Planetarium where the sub-Commission was holding its hearings. The building was surrounded by policemen and plainclothesmen who served to prevent any "unauthorized" persons from contacting the sub-Commission. The priest managed to get as far as a Cypriot interpreter and a young German staff member of the Secretariat. They told him that he would definitely not be heard. He asked if he could bring a statement. They asked him how long it would take to make it, and he said he would have it "in a minute." He went out to the *papadia,* who had his declaration hidden in her bodice. He came back and the Commission thus received his declaration.

On the 21st of April, 1969, the second anniversary of the military coup, Father Petros walked into St. George Church in Aghios Thomas. Amid the ikons was a photo of George Papadopoulos. He took the large photo out into the courtyard. There it was burned. Father Petros and others were arrested, but he was later released from jail when the public prosecutor said that a photo is not allowed in a church beside the ikons and the indignation of a priest was comprehensible under the circumstances.

COSTAS FRANTZESKAKIS—Accountant

Costas Frantzeskakis was born forty-seven years ago on the island of Milos, the Aegean island of the Cyclades group where the famed Venus de Milo was found. For almost half of these forty-seven years Costas Frantzeskakis has been either in the resistance or in prison. His is the story of a generation of left-wing Greeks. From 1941 to 1944 he was in the resistance movement against the Germans, a member of EPON, the communist-backed Panhellenic Youth Organization. He was arrested as a communist in 1947 and sent to the concentration camp on the island of Makronisos. It was here that communists were "rehabilitated." To force him to sign a declaration renouncing his political beliefs, his jailers tortured him. He refused to sign. He was moved to the detention camp of Aghios Efstratios and was kept there until 1961.

After he was released, he worked as an accountant. He had gone to high school in Piraeus and was a graduate of Athens University in the Faculty of Economics and Commerce. When he began work again he was active in the trade union movement and in the EDA party. A member of the Accountants Union (Piraeus Branch), he was elected a union representative to the Piraeus Trade Union Congress in 1965.

From the very first day of my arrest (25.8.67) until I was deported to Leros I was held in solitary confinement in the cells of Security Headquarters in Piraeus. Any communication with my relatives was strictly forbidden. In the beginning I had no food, no clothes, no blankets. I remained unshaven for a month and a half. I received my clothes in Leros and I was allowed to have blankets forty days later on the 3.10.67. From the 25.8.1967 until the 16.10.1967 I had to suffer a lot. I was allowed to eat properly for the first time on the seventeenth day after my arrest. The first twelve days I had to rely on the yoghurt to be found in the "Asphalia" (Security Police Headquarters) and the days after I could eat nothing because my stomach would not tolerate any more the yoghurt diet.

They beat me with thick twisted cables on the naked soles of my feet (the torture known as "falanga") and then they beat me on my whole body until I lost consciousness. This was done by a team of torturers (Foteinos, Iliopoulos, Kanatas and others) under the guidance of police officer Yannoutsos following orders of the head of the department Sotiris Kouvas. These tortures were done in conjunction with the interrogation. Before starting every torture session they first made sure that I was able to walk once more and the sessions lasted from half an hour to three hours, with intervals of about ten minutes. Because of these tortures I started to urinate blood and pus. My stomach—after the beating I got—would not accept any food at all.

For ten days I was vomiting, together with blood, whatever I was trying to swallow. (I had previously undergone a stomach operation.) Before and after the beating I was called to the office (on the whole I was called about twenty times) and was interrogated. They followed closely my physical and mental condition to see whether I was showing any signs of weakening. The interrogation always followed the same line. There were insults, threats and various "arguments" drawn from so-called evidence from the archives of the police. I was repeatedly threatened with court martial. Many times while I was being interrogated the telephone rang and my name was mentioned. I was pressed to inform on people, to change my beliefs because, as I was told, "your party will never lift its head again." "Now we have a revolutionary right and that is why we treat you in this way. We will not send you to the Royal Commissioner, we will interrogate you as long as we please. But even if this government goes you will continue to suffer like this as long as there is NATO." They also finished the sessions regularly by making the same proposal (or threat): "You will not come out of this alive unless you agree to become one of our agents." It seems that all these conversations were recorded by a hidden microphone in the room.

Finally they took a written statement from me for the Royal Commissioner (Public Prosecutor). As I was unable to move and continued to urinate blood and pus, they sent me—in order to recover—to Kallipolis Police Station (Commanding Police Officer Athanasios Hadjis). It was there that the Police doctor named Kappos visited me for the first time after police officer Kouvas finally gave his consent. I had repeatedly asked for the police doctor, previously to no avail, however. This police station had been converted into a secret nursing home for tortured people. There were three daily visits by the doctor while the officer on duty and the policemen were acting as male nurses putting hot towels on the beaten feet, themselves giving anti-vomiting medicine as well as other pain-relieving drugs and general care. The opinion of a high-ranking doctor that I should get proper treatment in a hospital was not followed. As soon as I was transferred to Leros I was hospitalized on the very same day in the "Aslipion," because my condition was very serious. I had lost twenty kilos and was in a state of complete exhaustion. As, however, the signs of my torture were as yet quite apparent, half an hour before the doctors of the International Red Cross visited the ward of the exiles, they took me away under the pretext that I had to undergo a neurological examination at the Leros hospital for mental diseases, so that the doctors could not see me. This was done without the knowledge of the medical authorities of the "Asclipion" under whose care I was. This fact was brought to the knowledge of the doctors of the IRC on the very same day that it happened. I am now in the camp of Partheni in Leros and my state of health is still very shaky.

Frantzeskakis

When Frantzeskakis wrote this he was a political prisoner in the Partheni camp on the island of Leros. He was later moved to Averoff prison in Athens. In May of 1969 after the Committee of Ministers of the Council of Europe decided not to expel Greece, there were seven political trials in one week. Eighteen prisoners, among them Frantzeskakis, were moved out of Averoff to Larissa, a city in north central Greece. They were not given sufficient notice to warn their families. There they were court-martialed, though none of them was from Larissa but from Crete and Piraeus. He has now been sentenced again.

Costas Frantzeskakis is married. His wife is in a detention camp. They have no children.

DIONYSIOS LIVANOS—Newspaperman

Dionysios Livanos was born on February 12, 1934. He was born into the Establishment and had a promising future as a member of it. At the university he studied political science, and politics were to be his main interest when the finished his studies. He once published a small right-wing daily newspaper called *Niki* and was active in politics as a member of ERE, the conservative party in Greece. He is the nephew of the wife of Panayiotis Canellopoulos, who is the head of the ERE party and was the Prime Minister at the time of the coup d'etat.

I was arrested on Good Friday, April 19, 1968. To be arrested on this Holy Day was something I would not have believed possible. I had just come back from Church in the evening. There were three friends at home, former General Vervoulakos, his wife, and a former Minister. Just before midnight there was a knock on the door. An army major in uniform named Anagnostopoulos came in, followed by a young army lieutenant Kakoyiannakos. The major asked, "Who is Livanos? " He ordered me to follow them. As I went out the door I saw soldiers in the garden with automatic weapons trained on my house. They got to their feet, grabbed me and put me up into an army truck. We then drove for half an hour. Nobody spoke.

We arrived at Aghia Paraskevi. Finally I asked where we were going. I was told that someone wanted to see me. I saw there was no point in asking anymore, but I was worried.

The truck drove through a grove of pines and came to a stop at a military checkpoint. There everybody got off and I was led to a near-by shed.

I found myself face to face with a Lieutenant Colonel and four other senior officers who were seated at a table at one end of the room. They stared at me. I just stood there. Finally the Lieutenant Colonel, Nicolas Dertilis, looked past me to the major, who was in the doorway, "Where did you pick up this wretch?" The Lieutenant Colonel got up. Major Avaliotis shouted, "Speak!"

"I don't understand."

"Speak!"

"I don't understand. I don't know why I am here."

"Speak !"

"I don't know what you want me to say."

Then he let forth terrible insults and shouted at me "Speak! " I kept repeating that I didn't understand what he wanted and what it was all about. He began to hit me in the head, beating me with his fists and with the flat of his hand. The others were saying, "Come on, out with it, let's finish. You might as well save your neck, speak! " I could only ask what it was they wanted me to tell. He kept hitting me and I was knocked to the floor. The Colonel would grab me by the shirt front, pick me up, and hit me again until I was knocked down once more. Then he gave an order which I couldn't understand. A soldier brought in a thick rope, a big cable and a bucket of water. By that time I felt very dizzy from the punches on my head, and I couldn't comprehend what these things were for. I remember very little. I remember being dragged away though I don't know by whom. It must have been three or four in the morning that I was dragged to the far end of the camp to a small building where they threw me into a dark cell. It had a cement floor and there was a small hole in the door from which I could just make out the soldier who guarded me. The soldier gave me his overcoat because it was so cold, but he was not. allowed to speak to me. I was unable to sleep. There was nothing to do but wait.

When the morning came I was led back to the same office. I waited there for almost three hours. Finally the Lieutenant Colonel came in and started the whole thing again. He insulted me, insulted Canellopoulos, Andreas Papandreou and started hitting me. Somehow this second session didn't affect me as much as I was so exhausted I was numb. I was taken back to the cell.

At six that evening a black car came for me with two civilians in it. I had to sign something for the duty officer. We drove for about an hour up the Attica Peninsula. There I was taken to a place. They put a paper in front of me. They didn't let me read it or even touch it, I had no idea what it was. They forced me to sign it, my hand moved without my wanting it.

I was turned over to the Security Police of Nea Ionaia.

By then I was a real convict, they took everything from me, my tie, my wallet, my shoelaces, my belt. I was led downstairs and put in a solitary confinement cell. There were other prisoners down there, one of them was Colonel Papaterpos. The pipe for the sewage had broken, and the sewage overflowed into the cells. For five days there was almost two inches of sewage in the corridors and in my cell. I was not allowed to go to the toilet. There was nothing to lie on and I had no blanket. I stayed there for sixteen days. In the cell next to me one man had a fever of forty degrees (104°F.) because of the wet conditions in his cell.

Every couple of days I would ask someone "Why am I here? " Nobody knew. "What are they going to ask me to do? " Nobody could answer. Finally my wife came and saw me. From the moment of my arrest she had been running from office to office trying to find out what had happened to me. They kept putting her off, saying that they didn't know. But finally she found out where I was being held, and she managed to come to see me. The gendarmerie was decent about visits.

I was having trouble with my ear because of the beatings. Even now, fourteen months later, I have dizzy spells and I cannot hear well. A young doctor came to see me in my cell. It is my left eardrum that is affected, but he only gave me aspirins as the police did not allow me to tell him what had happened. Later a private doctor appeared, but with five army officers. I was taken to a hospital and they examined me, but I never knew what the results were.

On May 6 they said that I was to be freed. Instead they took me to Maroussi. At least there I had a bed and there were others, such as the former Ministers George Rallis and George Mavros, and the former President of the Parliament, Papaspyrou. I was three and one half months there, and was never questioned. My wife and son were first allowed to see me twice a week and then only once a week. We had new arrivals, General Kollias, Admiral Spanides, Air Commodore Mitsakos, Brigadier Rouggeris, Mr. Kavounides, a Center Union politician, and Mr. Mothnios. When I was there I spoke to a delegate of the Red Cross.

On August 10th I was sent to the island of Parga. The order read only, "On the decision of the Ministers of Justice and Public Security, Mr. Dionysios Livanos is exiled." I was not allowed to say a word to anyone on the island. I couldn't even greet my fellow exiles, Brigadier Rougeris and General Koumanakos.*

Exile was a disaster for me financially. I had to pay to stay in a small hotel where they kept a constant eye on me and charged quite a lot. Twice a day I had to go to the police station to sign in.

They let me free in October and I was taken to Papaspyropoulos and Lambrou who warned me that I should not attempt to leave Greece.

I have never known why I was arrested, why I was beaten, why I was imprisoned and exiled, or why I was released.

The European Commission of Human Rights summoned Livanos as a witness in Greece. The Greek government named Captain John Vassilakopoulos of the 521st Marine Battalion to give evidence on this case. The captain testified that the reason Livanos was brought to the Marine camp was to "make representations to him not to hold meetings in his house and not to slander the army. Our representations were mainly meant to protect him, and make him not turn against the state. . . . the Director left, whilst we, the other officers remained in the office and held a rather friendlier discussion with Mr. Livanos, exchanging our views."

Since he was released, Livanos has been unable to find work, as the professions are closed to him. He now lives in the old family house in Kifissia, a suburb of Athens, with his wife and three-year-old son.

CONSTANTINE MELETIS—Tradesman

In October of 1968 Constantine Meletis received a thick letter from Strasbourg that had been sent to his home in Salonika through the Greek Ministry of Interior. Meletis, a thick-set man of thirty-eight, had been working as a salesman since his release from prison on July 24th. Two-thirds of his resistance group remained in prison,

*General Koumanakos was famous as the Commanding Officer of the Greek Contingent in Korea.

while the rest were released to be prosecution witnesses. The police spread the rumor that those who were released had betrayed their comrades. There was a cloud over Meletis; why indeed, the resistance asked, had he been freed?

He himself did not know how he had been caught in the first place until he learned in prison that the girl who had his telephone number had been arrested by the police. Her name was Kali Gavala, and in prison Meletis was told that she had been interrogated naked for nine hours and then put in a helicopter and dangled over Thermaikos Gulf from an iron cable, lifted up and down over the sea. They got his telephone number, and they got him.

Meletis thought the letter from Strasbourg, full of papers in a foreign language, had to do with business. He had it translated. Then he went to the police. The police told him that he might be sent to Strasbourg in France at the expense of the Greek government. There he would "defend the honor of his country." The police said, "You must say that you were not mistreated—that you were treated very well. Don't be afraid, because the judge will be in the Greek Embassy in Strasbourg. You will have guards with you from here, as well as legal help."

On Thursday, November 21, Meletis and his fiancee, Georgia Pangopoulo, who had been arrested with him, left Salonika for Athens with a police officer, Basilis Stamatelopoulos. It was a friendly enough trip (after his release from prison, Meletis had been cultivating the police in the hope that he would find a way to escape from Greece). They slept in a hotel in Athens. The next morning they went to Bouboulinas Street and presented themselves to Inspector Basil Lambrou, whom Meletis was meeting for the second time.

At the same time that Meletis was receiving his letter in Salonika, a man in Athens named Pandelis Marketakis was summoned to appear before Major Favatas, the director of the gendarmerie of Attica. Marketakis, a mechanic, was a shy man of thirty-six who looked ten years older. He lost an eye fighting the communists during the Civil War and suffers from an ulcer. Favatas gave him his telephone number, 298-122, explaining that it was for Marketakis's wife to get in touch with him if she needed any money for herself or the children. Marketakis would be leaving Greece for an international trial where the mother country was being accused of torture. He would go there and say that he had been well treated; even if he had been beaten up, this was between "us Greeks" and was not the business of foreigners. He just had to say that prisoners in Crete had not been tortured, that they had been well treated, had been allowed visits, and had gotten plenty of exercise. If he said this he would be protecting his country. It was not Germans or Russians or other foreigners who had beaten him up, and he was obligated to protect Greeks. He would have to refute any accusation that the Greek government was a dictatorship and say that the revolution was a revolution for the people. If he obeyed, he would get a promotion in his job, he would have direct access to Mr. Pattakos, and the Greek government would pay for a doctor and the treatment of his sick child.

During the next month Marketakis was called to the police station more than ten times for long conversations with Favatas. Favatas said Marketakis would be paid his salary while away and that when he returned he would be given a better job in any city of Greece he chose. At first the major said Marketakis was free to be a witness or not, but then he added that if he refused, Favatas would have trouble keeping Marketakis's boss from firing him. On his last visit to the police station, Favatas warned him that he must be careful what he said, for there would be police on the trip who would report back everything. There also would be many important Greeks there, doctors, professors, and lawyers to testify that Greeks are not tortured, so he had to be up to the standard of these learned men. The major gave him 2,000 drachmas ($66), telling him to stay in his house until a car passed the next day to pick him up.

The next morning at 9 o'clock a white Volkswagen with an American license plate (Marketakis remembers it was yellow with black letters, beginning with DGT 37) arrived with two plain-clothesmen. They were *Asphalia* men from the station of Helliniko. He was driven to Bouboulinas Street and taken to the office of Inspector Lambrou. There he met Constantine Meletis.

The two men were again instructed what to say in Strasbourg. Lambrou told them as they left that Andreas Papandreou had been about to make a coup and the army had saved Greece from hor-rible bloodshed.

Meletis and Marketakis were driven to the airport together on Saturday morning, November 23, in a civilian car. There they were given a group passport for four people. The third person was Miss Tsaira Peta, a young woman who came accompanied by Security Officer Babalis. The fourth person, Melfos, never appeared. Two policemen escorted them to the door of the Olympic Airways flight to Paris to join eight other Greeks headed for Strasbourg, in-cluding Nicolas Gournias, a torturer from the *Asphalia* of Boubou-linas Street.

When they landed in Paris, Dr. Kapsakis, Chief State Coroner, handled all the passports and filled out the forms. Marketakis and

Meletis had little chance to see the City of Light as they went to the air terminal and then straight to the railway station. Waiting for them in Strasbourg was Ambassador Vitsaksis, the junta's most ardent supporter on the foreign diplomatic scene, who was charged with the defense of the junta before the European Human Rights Commission. When Marketakis helped to unload the luggage from the Greek Embassy's white Triumph, he saw a rifle with a telescopic sight in the back of the luggage compartment.

Saturday night they went out to eat dinner at the Restaurant Diligence. There the delegation ran into Andreas Papandreou and a group of antijunta Greeks. There was some confusion on both sides, and a few insults, but neither was going to leave because of the other. Marketakis couldn't eat his food as he knew that Gournias, Krissikopoulos, and Manoulopoulos were carrying pistols and he was afraid they would shoot Papandreou. Yet Papandreou's presence gave Marketakis hope that there would be a way to escape. Papandreou, quite by accident, had reserved a room in the same hotel as the junta delegation, the Maison Rouge.

Sunday morning Meletis and Marketakis sat in the bar lounge with other witnesses and their guards, playing cards and drinking coffee. A man with glasses, a Greek, came up to them and began to chat in a friendly way. By the way he talked, and by the fact that he mentioned Papandreou, Meletis thought this was a Greek who might help. The group went into the hotel dining room to eat, and when they had difficulty reading the menu, the friendly Greek helped them. Marketakis said that he wanted to get cigarettes at the desk, and when he passed the man, he put a finger to his lips and then put his wrists together as though they were manacled.

Toward the end of the meal, Meletis got up to go to the bathroom. There he wrote a note for the Greek with glasses. "I see that you are an honest man and a right-thinking Greek. I would like to speak with you privately." At this moment Marketakis came into the bathroom. They had never spoken openly to each other. Meletis didn't trust Marketakis because he had a wife and two children in Greece and knew that he would have to speak the way the police had told them to. And Marketakis didn't trust Meletis. As they talked, they suddenly realized that they both had the same goal—escape. Meletis expressed his doubt about Marketakis because of his family problem. Marketakis said, "Look, if you don't trust me! " He turned over his coat lapel to reveal a pin of Eleftherios Venizelos, the great liberal statesman from Crete. With great relief the two men embraced each other. Quickly they discussed plans of how they would get away and how they could get the passport. They still believed that they would be testifying in the Greek Embassy. Meletis suggested that Marketakis get the guards out of the hotel so he could speak to the man with glasses.

Meletis announced that he had drunk too much wine and wanted to go up to take a siesta. He shook hands with the man with glasses, slipping him the note. Marketakis said he wanted to go over the border to Germany to buy something for his wife, as he heard things were cheaper there. His guards were reluctant, but he joked with them about keeping him prisoner, and finally his two guards and another witness, Zervoulakos, a filmmaker, agreed to go for a bus ride to Germany, for which they would need the passports.

Meletis stayed at the window of his room and watched them cross the square below. He rushed downstairs and saw his man talking with some Greeks, but he didn't see any delegation guards. He went into the bathroom and a few moments later the man with glasses followed. Meletis burst out, "I don't know if you're a security man, if you're with the junta or for democracy. But I'm not afraid. If you're a man interested in restoring democracy to our country, please help me, because I want to help this commission." Meletis wrote down his name and room number. The man with glasses gave him his name, George Vandelis. They parted.

Meletis lay on his bed waiting. There was a knock on the door. When Vandelis came in, Meletis told him that he wanted to get out right away and tell the truth. Vandelis said it would be better if he stayed with the Greek delegation and when the moment came to testify he would tell the truth and ask for asylum. Meletis said he couldn't wait, it had to be now, he had to fight them directly. They went to the door and peered out, checking the corridor. Then, making sure they weren't being followed, they ran upstairs to the room of Andreas Papandreou. Meletis told his story to Papandreou, who promised to help him. Meletis went down to pack his bag, and then walked out of the hotel. He arrived at the Grand Hotel, where the Norwegian lawyers were staying and which was the informal center for the antijunta forces. Milling about the lobby all week were journalists, exiled Greeks, witnesses, and Scandanavian jurists.

Marketakis returned to the Maison Rouge in the late afternoon. There sitting in the lobby was the man with glasses who said that Papandreou "owed him money," had not shown up, and he wasn't going to wait any longer. Marketakis was scared the man would leave before they could speak, so he asked him to inquire at the desk in French about pills for Marketakis's ulcer. They went to the desk, where Vandelis handed the Cretan a note which read, "Meletis is safe in another hotel. You can join him if you wish." Vandelis said good-by and walked out into the street.

Marketakis's guard, Manoulopoulos, came up and said that the man with the glasses looked suspicious to him. Why didn't Marketakis go out in the street and see if the man was speaking out there with others? Marketakis said that he shouldn't do it. The guard urged him as it would be "less suspicious." Marketakis walked out. He approached the man with glasses and asked to be taken directly to Andreas Papandreou, otherwise he would go back into the Maison Rouge. They stepped into a waiting car and drove off to the Grand Hotel.

Thus the day before the first hearings of "L'Affaire Grecque" were to begin, two key witnesses brought from Greece had bolted and were asking the Norwegians for sanctuary. For the Norwegians the arrival of the witnesses [on French territory] posed certain problems yet there was never any doubt that the two should be helped. From the standpoint of the case, the lawyers were anxious not to give the junta any excuse to pack up and leave. This was to be a persistent fear on the part of the Scandinavians, that the junta Greeks would pull out, and for this reason the Scandinavians were often to hold back their strongest cards.

The small conference room of the Grand Hotel held an excited group of lawyers and Greek exiles with Andreas Papandreou. Meletis had just told his story and said how glad he was to be out of that "horrible nightmare." Marketakis was saying he would have committed suicide before he would have spoken against *his* Greece. But, on the other hand, he was a husband and a father. With tears in his eyes he showed the picture of his wife and children and pleaded with the Scandanavians to do something to protect them.

The rumor of the escape had begun to travel about the hotel, but it was decided that the escapees should not speak to the press until after they had testified to the Commission, as that might constitute a provocation for the junta delegation to use as an excuse to decamp. The Norwegians immediately called the Secretary of the Commission so that he could come to discuss the matter. The Secretary said he could not come himself, as he was invited to a dinner party. The French police were informed, and a man in a trenchcoat materialized outside the hotel to walk up and down in the damp November chill of Strasbourg.

On Monday morning the first hearings of the Greek case began at the modern Commission building outside of Strasbourg, next door to the main building of the Council of Europe. The atmosphere was tense. This was the most important case the Commission had ever faced; the issue was not an obscure point of legal procedure interesting only to specialists. It was a question of suffering human beings, and it could be said without too much exaggeration that it had importance for all Europeans.

The witnesses were briefed inside the hearing room about the procedure of the hearings. They were held *in camera,* and nothing that went on in the hearing room could be told to anyone. Outside in the corridors, Greek security policemen paraded around with pistols barely concealed under their coats. Watching their every move were plainclothesmen of the French Surete, attached to the Council of Europe. From time to time a lawyer or a Commission official would come rushing out of the hearing room and there would be a whispered consultation in the hallway. Ambassador Vitsaksis had appeared in the morning with the "no comment" of a diplomat still awaiting instructions. The junta delegation, short and swarthy men who moved about in a gesticulating convoy during intermissions, contrasted with the tall pale Scandinavians. Outside the press waited, stamping their feet in the cold.

Before the first witness, Andreas Papandreou, was heard, there was the procedural problem of the two escaped witnesses. Would they still be heard? The Greeks argued that they had been their witnesses and now the delegation did not want them to be heard. The Commission held that each witness had been summoned by the Commission, thus they were Commission witnesses rather than the witnesses of one party. Therefore they would be heard.

Back in the hotel Marketakis broke down with an ulcer attack in the middle of giving his deposition. A doctor was called and ordered complete rest and no nervous excitement.

Tuesday afternoon a telephone call came to Room 509 of the Grand Hotel. A man, who would not give his name, said that he wanted to help the two witnesses return to the Greek delegation before they spoke. He said it was for "humanitarian interests." The man agreed to come to the hotel to talk about it. He went into Room 510 and spoke with the exiled Greek he had called. He said that his name was Konstantelos and he was a KYP man attached to the Greek Embassy in Paris. He was clearly upset, and said that he had come from Paris just "to save" the witnesses. When he was told the witnesses were free to choose and didn't seem in danger, he said that he really meant he wanted to save their families. He said that if they made a story that the Scandinavians had taken them at gunpoint, then he would guarantee their safety and the future safety of their families. The man refused to see the witnesses, but wanted the message conveyed to them. The man left, demanding an answer by that evening. Someone had carelessly left a tape recorder on in the room where the agent of the Greek intelligence agency had spoken. The tape was played to the two escapees and they were asked if they wanted to go back. They were hurt that anyone could doubt their sincerity and furious that anyone had agreed to talk to a junta man.

Speculation began to grow about the fate of a third witness, Miss Tsaira Peta. Journalists who went to the Maison Rouge to try to get the junta side of the story said she was in tears at dinner on Sunday, and any time she appeared out of her room she was flanked by two men. One journalist, trying to find out about her, had been roughed up by Greek security policemen. She had been visibly shaken when she went to the Commission building and saw Kitti Arseni, who had been in the *Asphalia* at the same time she was. By Tuesday she had disappeared. Some reports had her in the Greek Embassy in Paris, as the French Police implied she couldn't have left France without their knowing it. At week's end she appeared in Athens. In any case, she never testified. The Greek Delegation gave three different reasons for her precipitous return to Athens: she was sick, her sister was sick, the pressure of business commitments forced her return. Miss Peta is a seamstress.

The Commission said that it would hear the two witnesses, Meletis and Marketakis, Wednesday morning. They left Room 510 under the glaring lights of TV camera crews and accompanied by the Danish lawyer, Ole Espersen, they descended in the glass-enclosed elevator to the lobby. They got into a taxi, and with French Surete cars in front and behind, they threaded their way through the streets of Strasbourg, over the canal, past the university to the Commission building. They walked up the crowded steps, confronted for the first time members of the Greek delegation, and walked on to the room where the witnesses waited to be called.

Meletis was the first to take the oath, and he had a story to tell that was not the one the Greek lawyers and security policemen in the delegation planned. The change in situation was dramatized by the fact that Gournias, a torturer, sat in the delegation with a pistol in his pocket and could do nothing to silence Meletis. It was not as Meletis and Marketakis had been told in Greece, "The foreigners, members of the Commission, will be in the Greek Embassy to listen to the witnesses rebuff the slanders of the enemies of Greece."

> I was involved with the resistance from May of 1967 when I gave refuge in my room to a man who was hunted by the police. [Since testimony before the Commission is secret, it is not possible to know exactly what Meletis said.

This, however, is his story and one can assume that he gave in substance the same account.] His name was Alexandros Iossifides, a lawyer and Salonika borough Councillor who was a former political prisoner who had never signed the loyalty declaration. There aren't many around who have been able to avoid doing that. Iossifides got caught later, and he jumped out the window of the Asphalia. When I was there a policeman told me that Iossifides could not stand the new methods of torture. While he was in the toilet he asked his guard to get some toilet paper, and while the guard was away, he jumped. [Iossifides survived this leap, although at his trial in June, 1969, he was still on crutches, having suffered multiple fractures.]

I was arrested at two o'clock in the morning on May 8, 1968. I was driving a rented Volkswagen to Athens with George Tsarouchas, who was a member of the last Parliament, George Mastoras and Georgia Pangopoulou. Both Mastoras and Tsarouchas were in hiding and were wanted by the police. Both of them had heart trouble and I was driving them to Athens as that was the only place they could see a doctor. We passed the first highway toll station at Katerini on the Salonika-Athens highway. Eight cars pulled out to follow us. After about five hundred meters a police car forced us to the side of the road and a car with civilian plates passed alongside and started shooting. We stopped. Men banged at the door and the windows with their guns. We were dragged out of the car. One of the policemen hit me in the face with his Thompson sub-machine gun, breaking my cheekbone. They pulled out Tsarouchas, threw him to the ground and two policemen kicked him in the crotch. Ten people were beating us. Mastoras was crying, "Please don't beat me, because I am ready to die."

We were put in three different cars to be taken to the Third Corps Headquarters in Salonika. In the car on the way they beat me trying to make me talk. They beat me with the Thompson, insulting me all the time, and asking me why I was driving Tsarouchas. When we reached the Axios river they stopped the car and took me out, saying, "If you don't talk, we'll throw you in." I could see that the people in the other two cars were getting the same treatment. As a result of all this, Tsarouchas never reached Salonika alive.

We were put in separate rooms in the Third Corps. I found that two of my friends were there, and I could hear the police beating them. They were Theodoros Kazelis and Baras. I could hear their voices.

A man came into my room who probably was from KYP. He demanded that I write a curriculum vitae. When I had written it, he smiled ironically as he read it. Then they asked me to write a confession, giving the names and addresses of the people with whom I worked. I did not.

They told me, "You see this safe? Go, close, and see all the testimony against you." I went to look and they closed the door on me so that my neck was caught and they pushed on it. A short man said, "You fairy! You'll speak or we'll kill you! "

More people came into the room, they crowded around me, all making dirty and ironic remarks. About ten or twelve men started to beat me, all at the same time.

From the next room I could hear something I will never forget. I think it was Baras. They were beating him so much that I could hear him vomiting, but in such a way that he sounded like an ox. This Baras had been in a legal strike before April 21 which ended in a demonstration. They had nothing legal against him in peacetime, but now they had their chance and they took him.

A captain of the gendarmerie of Salonika, named Stamatotpoulos, came in the room. I lifted up my shirt to show that I had had an operation and if they beat me again there was a danger that my intestines would come out and I would die. They then put me on the floor and the chief said something to the others. They went out, but a guard remained next to me.

The next day I was taken to the Asphalia building. There I always had two guards with me. Water, food and cigarettes were strictly forbidden. I was taken to the second floor of the building where there was a group waiting to interrogate me. Among others there was a Lieutenant Diplas, there was a three-star officer who is the chief of the Third Police Station in Salonika, and the prosecutor, who is a ridiculous person. They interrogated me on the Tsarouchas case and from their questions I guessed that Tsarouchas might be dead. The small man asked me, "Tsarouchas suffered from his heart, isn't that so? " They made a document about Tsarouchas which they made me sign without seeing it properly. When they left I realized that Tsarouchas was dead.

After the interrogation I was thrown into a cell at the Third Police Station of Salonika. The man that received me there was Gendarme Lieutenant Tetradakos. The same day I was taken out and down the stairs. I was led to the street, across from the police station. There was a little restaurant called "Perdica" and the students there saw me. The guards threw me into a car and the officer told me that if I didn't speak today, I would die. I was taken again to the main building.

They took me to a large room where there were small tables and they began asking me questions. When I didn't answer they started saying terrible things about my mother and my fiancee, very personal things. I was put in a room which was separated by a curtain and told to take my shoes off. I was forced to lie on a bed with a mattress. They made me place my hands so that I could not protect my vulnerable area. I was tied to the bed with electric cords. They had a little machine which produced a current and they put the wires on my toes and fingers.

At the same time I was getting these electric shocks, they beat me. They put a towel on my face so no marks would be left when they beat me there. Finally they gave me electric shocks on my genitals. The persons in the room were Karamitsos, Tetradakos, Mestromaras and Mitsou, as well as four more.

After one hour of torture, Tetradakos said to me, "Now, since you don't speak, we will take you to the Bulgarian frontier and shoot you there. We will say that you tried to escape to Bulgaria." They stopped the electric shocks. My feet were still tied. They put handcuffs on me in such a way that I couldn't move my hands at all. I was left on the bed for another half an hour. Then they slipped a black sack over my head so that I couldn't see anything. I was put in a car. They seemed to drive around Salonika. Again they told me that I would be shot at the frontier, but I was quite sure we were still in Salonika.

I was led to a military shack which had the look of an abandoned place, there was only a kerosene lamp inside. They put me down on the cement floor. They took a rifle and wound the strap around my ankles, then I was hoisted up in the air and they beat the soles of my feet.

After some time I no longer had the sense of pain. They threw water on the cement floor and ordered me to jump on the floor so that sensation would return to my numb limbs. The sensation came back and the beating was more painful the next time. They also beat me on the calves of my legs. After I was taken back to the Third Police Station and thrown in a cell.

In the night something happened that I will never forget. The night guard spoke to me in a friendly way and told me to have courage, "It will pass." He asked me if I wanted a cigarette, but said that if I heard steps to put it in the hole in the cement floor. This is the one kind incident I remember.

I was taken to some place outside Salonika and made to stand in front of an open grave. Just before I was to be shot, someone ran up and said, "Don't shoot him! He's all right, he'll tell you the names of the others!" I knew it was a trick and that it was only a mock execution. They made me get in and out of the grave. I was picking thorns out of my body for three days after that.

Finally I broke down and talked. There were eight people beating me continuously. I signed something. I did not understand why I was signing it. After that I was taken to Athens by plane. I had two guards, Stamatelopoulos and Komporozos. At the airport I was given food, my first in three days.

I was taken to the Asphalia building in Athens to Inspector Lambrou. They put me in a cell next to a cell where they were torturing. I could hear voices calling out in despair. It was terrible to hear those cries. They didn't beat me in the Asphalia.

I was put in a little room with three others, there was just enough room for us to sit down, there was no fresh air and as it was summer it was very hot. I was able to lie next to the door to get some air that came through the one-centimeter space between the door and the floor. My ear became badly inflamed, and I was taken to the military hospital. I stayed in the Asphalia for ten days and could hear the sound of a machine used to cover the screams. They put sandbags on my stomach so they could start beating me again without leaving any marks.

Finally I was sent back to Salonika. I went through different cells and different prisons. In the Sixth Police

Station I met a man, Yiannis Grigoriadis, a student, who even though he had *falanga* seventy-nine days before, you could still see the marks on his feet.

I was imprisoned from May 9 to July 10, 1968. I was released and named as a witness for the prosecution.

When Meletis came back to the witness room, he could not keep back a big smile. Now Marketakis was called. The moment had come.

I was living in Chania in Crete at the time of the coup, and I was working as a car mechanic at the Royal Naval Station of Chania. On July 7, 1967, I was arrested at about ten in the morning. I was taken to Chania Security Headquarters and there Kapellou talked nicely to me and said that they knew all about the distribution of pamphlets. If I gave information about the others, I would be allowed to go back to work, all I had to do was give my contacts. I said that I didn't belong to any organization and therefore I didn't expect anyone to be contacting me. Finally they let me go that same evening and I went home. I went regularly to work for five days though I noticed that I was continually followed and watched, even during my working hours.

On the fifth day, at five o'clock in the morning, five security policemen came to the house. They ordered me to come with them and they took me in a police car to the Security Headquarters. I was led to Kapellou's office where the interrogation began.

"Are you a member of the Patriotic Front? "

"No."

"Do you know of other members of the Patriotic Front in Crete aside from Brillakis, Dr. Archondrakis and Gazis? "

"I don't know of anyone and I don't know anything about this organization."

At this point Kapellou started kicking me in the face, the chest and the stomach. Another Asphalia member, Georgopoulos, was standing by. He started insulting me, calling me a "Bulgarian," and threatening to kill me if I didn't help with the interrogation. I was kept there for two days, interrogated at intervals. During interrogation I was hit by Kapellou who asked me about a mimeograph machine which was found at Kalanzandonakis's house. I refused to answer, and the blows became heavier and heavier.

After these two days, I was transferred to Mettagogon. There I was put in a room with eighteen other men, who were accused of either distributing pamphlets or having illegal meetings in Chania. I was kept there for twenty days. For eight days I received no food. Water was given to me by the guard in the evening. Each day the officers of the prison came and said that food would be given only to those who gave names and information.

During this time at the transfer place, Paul Brillakis showed me his blackened bruised body. The Asphalia during two days of interrogation hit Brillakis with bags full of sand all over his body and with a wire rod on the soles of his feet. Brillakis's face was all bruised and caked with blood.

Gazis, a lawyer, was in solitary confinement for eight days during interrogation. He had been beaten up very badly and he was very weak because he had not received any food. Dr. Archondrakis had also been beaten up and had had his beard pulled out hair by hair during the interrogation. Nearly all the rest of them had been beaten up, but these three were the worst cases of torture. On the 27th of July, eight detainees were tried for resisting the emergency martial law, distributing pamphlets after having used illegally a mimeograph machine and because a revolver had been found in the doctor's house. I was set free because I did not have a file with the security police and I had not participated in distributing pamphlets.

When I was freed from prison, I learned that I had been fired from my job at the Royal Naval Base, as a "danger to the nation." I could not find a job anywhere. I was desperately in need of money to support my wife, child and new-born baby. I used to drive cars in exchange for something to eat.

On March 4, 1968, I was rearrested in Chania, accused of having participated in the explosion at the Chania electric power station. I was taken to the Asphalia of Chania where I was kept under interrogation for 75 days. It was hell.

During the first five days I was given neither food nor water, and they called me at all hours of night and day for interrogation. When I was interrogated I was beaten and kicked all over the body by several men at once who insulted me all the time. In my cell, it was impossible to lie down, I could only sit and I had to urinate and defecate there. I had no blanket and the floor was constantly wet.

One of the worst things for me was to be constantly woken up in this sitting position. In 1948 when I with my father and all my brothers had fought the Communists, I was wounded in the head. All the beating brought back the old trouble, I started to be dizzy and to have unbearable headaches.

After about thirty-five or forty days, I don't remember exactly, my ulcer began to hemorrhage. I had asked before this for a doctor but no doctor ever came. Finally when my wife and mother-in-law were allowed to visit me, I told them of my condition. When they left the Asphalia, they made a hysterical scene, falling on the pavement screaming that I would die because the police would not let a doctor see me. After that a doctor was sent and examined me. He told the police that if the torturing went on I would die, because my old head trouble was renewed and because of the nervous shock my stomach trouble was very serious.

I was sent to be X-rayed and the doctor verified that the hemorrhage had resulted from my terrible nervous condition caused by the type of torture I had suffered. Then I was given a mattress, and they stopped torturing me. On the 75th day I was transferred to the Chania prison.

I spent another two months in prison. There I met a priest, Petros Gavalas, with whom I shared a cell. The priest had been badly beaten, and you could still see even after so many days the marks and bruises. The priest told me that they had pulled out the hair from his beard and from his pubic area. My brother-in-law had been arrested at the same time. He was held 93 days in solitary confinement at the Chania station.

I left prison on June 24, 1968.

Marketakis returned to a witness room that was full of triumphant laughter and congratulations. Lawyers and witnesses talked alternately in excited and confidential tones between bites of ham sandwiches brought from outside. Throughout the week there had been tremendous solidarity among antijunta Greeks. Political enemies of the past even spoke to each other, and factional quarrels were put aside in a common effort to help the case. Scandinavians, getting into the spirit of the thing, began to have trouble restraining moments of Greek-like exuberance, and the Greeks, conscious of their reputation as emotional Mediterraneans, spoke at times with an anglo-saxon understatement befitting the juridical nature of the occasion.

Marketakis still had his bags at the Maison Rouge and the French Surete accompanied the two witnesses back to their former hotel. There they confronted the Greek delegation, led by Pelos Koutoupis. Meletis, flanked by French Surete, faced them and shouted in Greek, "'Fuck you, you fascists!" Koutoupis turned on Marketakis, "Your wife and children will pay for what you did today! "

Meletis and Marketakis returned to Room 510 of the Grand Hotel. Their room was full of Greek exiles, mostly from Germany. Marketakis's ulcer was giving him a great deal of pain. The full implication of what they had done was now sinking in. They had testified. They had told the truth. Now what? They broke out the whiskey.

The Norwegian trade unions offered to help, and a Norwegian journalist named Gerhardsson met with them in Marotis's room on the sixth floor and assured them they would have jobs and everything would be all right. The Norwegians would do all they could so that Marketakis could have his wife and children out. Marketakis was in tears and the two Greeks embraced the tall Norwegian.

Thursday Marketakis had a nervous collapse. He shouted and quarreled with everyone. On Friday the two witnesses appeared before the press with Andreas Papandreou. On Saturday they said good-by outside the Grand Hotel and drove off for the north in a black Mercedes.

Pelos Koutoupis, the head of the Greek delegation, finally gave a press conference in which he stated, "The two men were kidnapped, terrorized, and probably paid. They were the victims of a blackmail in the communist manner." Asked about his threat to Marketakis, he replied, "I am authorized to confirm that the families of the two kidnapped men are in no danger, but will be under the protection of the Greek authorities in order to avoid any threat like that to which they have been subjected in Strasbourg." [*The Times,* December 2, 1968.]

Everyone thought that this was the end of the story. It was not. Meletis went to work immediately as a butcher in Oslo, while Marketakis was admitted to a hospital. He was alone there, unable to speak a word of a foreign language. The few Greeks he had met all seemed to be Stalinists from the Civil War period, and he had fought the communists and was a Center Union man. The long winter nights were at their longest; there was no Cretan sun. His wife telephoned him—from the *Asphalia* in Athens—though no one knows what she said.

On December 15 he took a night train alone from Oslo to Stockholm. He was to be met at the station by a friend of Andreas

Papandreou but the man was late. When he did arrive there was
no sign of Marketakis. The police were informed, but for thirty-six
hours no one knew where he was. Finally the Greek Embassy in
Stockholm announced that he was there. Marketakis then told the
press that he had been "kidnapped by communists" and had "spoken
under the threat of twenty revolvers." He wanted to go back to
Strasbourg "to tell the truth."

The Commission was holding its second hearings the same week,
and from Strasbourg followed his odyssey from Stockholm to London
to Paris. In each capital he held a press conference and gave further
details. He had been struck down on a Strasbourg street corner and
taken to Andreas Papandreou and those other "Bolsheviks." Mr.
Evensen, the noted Norwegian international lawyer, who is in charge
of the Scandinavian case, had judo-punched him while Mr. Gerhardsson pinned his arms back. He had not dared to speak to the
Commission openly as the President of the Commission had paid
him 750 francs through Mr. Evensen and they were thus ac-
complices. (The Commission did give each witness travel and living
expenses.) The Commission decided that they would hear Marketakis alone without the lawyers of either side. Mr. Vitsaksis
protested.

Strasbourg braced itself, but Marketakis never came, flying on to
Athens instead. When he landed, Pattakos greeted him with a
chorus of relatives sobbing in the background. Marketakis shouted,
"Long Live Pattakos! Long Live the National Government! "

What happened still remains a mystery. Was he followed on the
train and kidnapped by a KYP man? Did he, as many believe, get
to the station to find no one there and get directed to the Greek
Embassy by a kindly Swede? Or had he already decided in Oslo
to go back to his family? Or was he an *agent provocateur* from
the very start. Only Marketakis knows the whole story. And maybe
now even he doesn't know, for to those who saw him in Strasbourg
it was clear he was a broken man.

Meletis passed a difficult winter in Oslo, especially because his
fiancée, Georgia Pangopoulou, was still in Greece. The police had
gone to her house and asked for recent photos of Meletis as well as
his phone number. They proposed that she lure him to Italy, "where
they were prepared for this kind of thing," and then they would
bring him back to her.

The Greek resistance helped her to escape and she was re-
united with Meletis in Oslo. For her also it was a difficult ad-
justment, and she left her family behind. In June she came to
testify at the Commission's last hearings. She told what she re-

membered of the Tsarouchas incident and about her tortures. Life in exile is still not easy.

Marketakis is reported to be doing well. The government has given him a small house where he lives with his wife and two children.

GERASSIMOS NOTARAS—Political Scientist

For four of the eight years Gerassimos Notaras lived in Lausanne, Switzerland, he got up at six in the morning, drove for an hour and a half to Bern, where he worked a full day at the Greek Embassy, drove back, arriving at eight o'clock, studied until twelve, then went out until three in the morning to talk with his friends. This strong constitution of his was to stand him in good stead, perhaps too good stead, as it was to take two different periods of prolonged torture and special effort to make him sign a "confession."

Notaras is the physical opposite of the short squat men who run Greece today. He is a lanky six-foot-four, and an aquiline nose and glasses contribute to his refined and earnest air. His family, from Trikala in the Peloponnesus, is well known as a landholding family that risked all its wealth to support the War of Independence against the Turks. The church there is called St. Gerassimos. His father was active in politics, a Venezelist, and at times held the post of nomarch, a government official, in various parts of Greece, though Gerassimos, the only child, lived most of his youth in Athens. He spent one year at the Polytechnical School in Athens, thinking he would be a physical scientist, but he left Greece in 1956 to study at the University of Lausanne.

His record was brilliant in Switzerland. Not only did he receive various academic honors, but he was active as a student leader. He was an assistant to political scientist Professor Jean Meynaud and collaborated on three books with him, most notably *Les Forces Politiques en Grece,* which has been translated into Greek and English. Though he came from a distinguished family, the family had little and was unable to send their son money for his studies. Notaras worked until his last two years when he received a scholarship from the Swiss Confederation (a rare honor for a foreigner) which enabled him to work full time on his doctoral dissertation. During these years he was not a politically committed person, but he maintained a strong interest in Greek affairs and like other students in Lausanne he followed the Algerian War closely through his contact with the many Algerians in Switzerland. Never did he consider staying abroad where he could have pursued any number of successful and remunerative careers; he always intended to go back to Greece where he would follow in the family tradition of politics and public service.

In 1965 his father died, and he had to return home. The next year he married a Swiss girl and they settled in Athens. Working as a Chief Researcher at the Center of Sociological Studies, he specialized in problems of emigration. He was attracted to the young team around Andreas Papandreou, and thought of running for Parliament under the aegis of the Center Union Party.

After the coup he joined Democratic Defense, the centrist resistance organization. He was active printing and distributing tracts, tracts quite moderate in tone. Their group was apparently discovered because a suspected printer was watched by the police. On October 28, 1967, the *Asthalia* came to the Center looking for him. A colleague, who now enjoys an important post in the Ministry of Health, telephoned Notaras and told him that he should come to the office. Friends of Notaras slipped out to the street to try to telephone a warning, but it was too late. He had already left the house.

He was taken to the *Asphalia* at Bouboulinas Street. He was six days in solitary confinement without food or water. He was taken to the terrace three times. He had *falanga,* mock executions, and was hung up by his hands bound behind his back. He was never charged nor allowed to contact a lawyer during his two months of detention. On the day of the "Christmas Amnesty," December 23, 1967, he was formally charged and moved to Averoff Prison. The political prisoners during this period were badly treated there, deprived of many rights such as the right to attend religious services and the right to use the library.

On the tenth of February Notaras disappeared from Averoff. His wife was told by the authorities that they didn't know anything about his case. The Athens grapevine soon spread the message that the laid-up warship, *Elli,* at the Scaramanga Naval Base opposite Salamis island was full of prisoners who were being tortured. On March 8, 1968, Notaras was returned to Averoff. His friends did not recognize him, he was barely able to walk, and he trembled and quivered uncontrollably.

On July 4, 1968, he was brought to trial, charged with con-
spiring with naval enlisted men to sabotage naval ships and to blow
up various installations. He catagorically denied this, telling the
court-martial:

> It is a fact that I have been a member of the Democratic
> Defense.
> It is a fact that I am opposed to the present government.
> However, my opposition to this government has not been
> motivated by the intention of overthrowing the established
> political and social order. My actions have been prompted
> by my profound belief in democracy, in human rights and
> freedom. I am convinced that it is precisely the violent
> conquest of power by a minority, which lends credence to
> the arguments of those who really wish to overthrow the
> social order. This usurpation of power lies outside of the
> framework of democracy, which framework forms the basis
> of the system in which I believe. I know that in com-
> mitting the acts which I committed, I placed myself out-
> side the realm of law, according to the rules which are in
> force at present. Nevertheless beyond this law, there is a
> natural law and a positive law. In accordance with natural
> law, I did what my conscience dictated and what I be-
> lieved to be in the interests of my country. In accordance
> with positive law, I acted in defense of the Constitution,
> obedient to my duty as a Greek, which required that I
> should help instill regard for its principles.

He then made a statement about what had happened to him on
the *Elli* and denounced his testimony as extracted under torture,
in open court with foreign observers present. Though this was later
to become a daily occurrence, his courage provided a dramatic
moment. The court did not contest his statement, but considered
it irrelevant.

> Declaration before the Extraordinary Court Martial of
> Athens:

> I do not admit the contents of my testimony made before
> the naval authorities (Captain Evangelopoulos, and others)
> on 18.2.1968 and 27.2.1968, given that the greater part of
> this was made as the result of physical and mental vio-
> lence exerted on me. In point of fact, on 10.2.1968, namely

at the time of the completion of the preliminary investigations by the Sub-Administration of the "Asphalia" of Athens, my case was referred to the Military Court of Athens and I was transferred to Averoff Prison. Two policemen admitted me and conducted me to New Perama where they handed me over to the Lieutenant Kiosses R.N., who was accompanied by two men of Chaser Submarine Command (D.Y.K.) and by a man unknown to me, wearing civilian dress. Subsequently I was taken to the naval ship "Elli,' which was out of commission, where the Lieutenant-Commander Kamarineas, R.N., and Major Theophiloyannakos of the Military Police were waiting for me. I remained under investigation in this ship from the above date (10.2.1968) until 8th March, 1968. Throughout this period I repeatedly suffered the "falanga" torture, which the two above-mentioned men of D.Y.K. applied to me.

Similarly I was repeatedly beaten throughout the duration of the investigation by these above-mentioned persons, as well as by members of the Naval Police, who, not satisfied with the above-mentioned beatings, came at night into the cell where I was held and beat me, demanding that I should admit and confess to the above-mentioned testimonies which I had supposedly made.

Because I had mental endurance and did not proceed to these confessions, they put me to the torture of electric shock, which was inflicted on me as I was stretched out and tied for hours on a metal spring mattress in a passage in the fore part of the ship.

In addition to all this they continually threatened that I should be drowned, as if by accident, if I did not confess.

Throughout all this time a high-powered electric light was burning in my cell so that I could not sleep and from time to time, for the same purpose, the guards beat noisily on the sheet-iron of my cell.

Finally I declare that I was never allowed to wash or smoke or read and only two glasses of water a day were allocated to me, with the object of weakening, in this way also, my physical and mental resistance so that I should confess all that my questioners demanded.

Consequently the so-called "depositions" or "testimonies" do not constitute the product of my free will. They were extracted as the result of the above tortures, consisting of intolerable, illegal and immoral physical and mental vio-

lence aimed at distorting my testimony on the subject of the
activities of Politis, my co-accused, and at adding other
acts which I had never committed and words which I had
never uttered.

Notaras was sentenced to eight years. He began his new imprisonment at Aegina prison in a cell with homosexual prisoners
who were encouraged by the authorities to molest him. His morale
was very low. Thanks to the intervention of the Red Cross and the
efforts of his many friends in Switzerland, he was moved to a cell
with other political prisoners. Though they spent a very difficult
and cold winter with the eighty political prisoners constantly sick,
the conditions are preferable to those of Averoff. He has a chair,
a desk, and the right to read and exercise. For a political prisoner
and an intellectual the conditions are not intolerable. (It has been
particularly difficult for his wife, who must work hard in order to
support herself and her mother-in-law.) The prisoners have organized a whole curriculum of courses at the "University of
Aegina." It is said that two weeks in Athens convinced one young
released prisoner that for his education it was better to return to
Aegina where the intellectual atmosphere was more stimulating and
free.

YIANNIS LELOUDAS — Poet, Archaeologist

November 15, 1967. The Military Tribunal of Athens. Thirty-one
members of the "Patriotic Front" face a court-martial of four military officers and a civilian judge. The thirty-second and most
celebrated defendant, Mikis Theodorakis, is not in the courtroom,
but in a prison hospital, "too ill to attend." The seventeen men and
fourteen women are charged with attempting to overthrow "the
existing regime and prevailing social order." Though the defendants are a diverse group socially and politically, ranging from
Right to Left, the prosecution maintains that they are all communists taking orders from Moscow. This is a political trial, and
it is clear to all that legal arguments are of no consequence, that
only political arguments count. Here—in the center of Athens in a

courtroom open only to security policemen, journalists, and relatives—is the one place in Greece where open political debate can
be heard. For the first time in a trial since April 21, the defendants
are given the right to speak, to make their *apologia*.

A young man of twenty-eight rises to face the judges. He speaks
in a calm, even voice, no gestures, no histrionics. "You say that it
is only the communists who are against you. I am not a communist,
and I am against you. It is precisely your kind, the Czars, the
Batistas, the Chiangs that bring communism." The military officers
on the bench erupt in shouts, "What about Czechoslovakia! What
about Hungary! " The young man answers in the same even, almost detached, tone. With each answer the fury of the khaki-clad
judges mounts to a point where it looks as though they will leap
on the accused. One is restrained only by the civilian judge, and
shouts, "The trouble with you is you were never in the army! "

The prosecutor, in a Vishinsky-style "mad dog" speech, has demanded a sentence of sixteen years. But this is a political trial, and
the sentences are measured not by evidence, but by attitude. "Re-
pentance" shortens the sentence; defiance lengthens it. The court-
martial sentences the young man to life imprisonment. His father, a
retired admiral, a conservative, and a royalist, receives the sym-
pathies of those around him after the verdict is announced.

Yiannis Leloudas came back to Greece in 1966 to do his military service after seven years of study in Paris. When he left
Paris, he was still working on his thesis at the Sorbonne, a study
of the first stone columns in India, he had translated Garcia Lorca
into Greek, and was a poet in his own right. His world was not the
world of politics. But the navy doctors detected a heart defect and
deferred him for a year.

When the coup came his immediate response was not to "wait
and see" but to do something. The next day, with his back turned
to the cameras, he was interviewed by three foreign television
stations. Four days later Mikis Theodorakis, the left-wing composer,
and Constantine Filinis, a highly respected communist leader who
has spent most of his adult life in prison, were hiding in his apartment. He became part of the resistance organization, "Patriotic
Front."

His affidavit was written in his own English.

> This document is intended to serve as testimony on the
> current and systematic use, by the Security Police and other
> agencies in Greece, of various methods of inflicting physical
> pain over a sustained period of time, of psychological in-
> timidation, of privations beyond the simple privation of

liberty, and of generally inhuman and degrading treatment, against opponents of the present Greek government. In it will be recounted, in some detail, my personal experiences at the hands of the Athens Security Police, and only such instances of the above as have been actually seen or heard by me.

(My name is Ioannis Leloudas, and I was arrested for anti-governmental activities on the evening of August 21, 1967, and subsequently condemned to life imprisonment.)

Immediately following my arrest, and having refused to disclose information which would have led to the capture of at least one of the people involved in the resistance network I worked for, I was threatened with execution on the spot. I was blindfolded and carried to the "spot," where, having waited for an amount of time which I am unable to calculate in terms of clock time, instead of the shot I expected, I started receiving blows all over my body, except those parts where the blows might have caused a bone to break, by means of a wooden log, which I felt to swell to unnatural proportions as the blows went on. I later understood that it was not the log which kept swelling with each blow, but my own body. (As I was still blindfolded, and wishing to awaken some sort of shame in my torturers, I asked them how many men it took to beat me up. Their reply which I consider significant, was: "Seven. You are a liar and we have the right to be seven to beat you up." As this indicated that they considered this quite a normal state of affairs.) I knew then that I had moved into another universe and that I could have no hope of the least communication on common human premises. From then on we both had very definite jobs to do: they to torture, and I to be tortured. Which is what happened for what I calculate to have been five continuous hours. Very soon the method of torture they resorted to was the "falanga." I was subjected to this basic and most widely used method of torture completely naked except for my underpants, gagged at times, when they thought that I was ready to scream my pain out, continuously menaced with further and more elaborate methods of torture, such as impalement, if I did not "talk," insulted with the foulest epithets in the Greek language, hit and kicked all over my body, including my stomach, testicles and face, even though they were very particular over not leaving any marks on my face, and finally shot at, at close range and close enough to make their menace of killing me plausible without touching me. My instinct of self-preservation managed at the time to persuade me that the shots fired were blanks, although now I cannot really believe that Security Police officers go around with pistols charged with blanks. There were twelve or thirteen persons actively involved in this, alternating as the one in charge of the feet got tired and relaxing by kicking and hitting wherever they found a spot where there was nobody hitting. Inspector Vassilios Lambrou, head of the so-called Information Department, Lieutenant Evangelos Mallios, assistant to Inspector Lambrou, and Lieutenant Petros Babalis, also assistant to the same, directed and actively participated in what everybody seemed to consider, and actually was, a normal and ordinary working session.

I have at this point to describe what the "falanga" consists of. The prisoner is made to lie on his back, and tied or held in that position, while he is being beaten on the soles of his feet by means of an iron or wooden rod for a period of time depending on his physical and moral resistance, the torturer or torturers' ability to stand the fatigue caused by his job, the importance of the questions asked, and the number of prisoners waiting to be treated. It is administered on shod feet, as shoes prevent the feet from being swollen to insensitivity or burst open after the first five or so minutes. Another measure usually taken towards the same end is making the prisoner stand up from time to time and made to walk or jump around, so that the muscles will work. It can be seen that the "falanga" presents numerous advantages, which have made it the favourite form of torture. It ensures maximum pain through a relatively unlimited time of full consciousness on the part of the prisoner. People very often faint or pray to faint, but they are immediately revived. It leaves no permanent marks such as scars or broken bones. One notable exception to this rule is Apostolos Dakos, who limped through Averoff Prison in December, 1967, the sole of his right foot burst open like an over-ripe fruit, the red and raw flesh visible even through his stockings, and two of his toe bones broken and crookedly mended through lack of medical help. Prisoners having been subjected to the "falanga" are able to walk normally and are presentable again in an interval of time which can extend from 10 days to much more, depending on the person's age and ability to recover. Ilias

Bentzelos still had to regularly bathe his feet in warm water three months after he had been tortured, as the soles were still of a bluish hue and still aching. I was able to walk in around fifteen days. The "falanga" can be administered once or repeatedly at a day's or more interval. The person being brought in after treatment is carried by two or more policemen, or in worse cases brought down in a blanket. He is usually in a state of consciousness comparable to somnambulism. A young boy, whose name I cannot disclose as I do not know his present whereabouts, two hours after he had been brought down, having completely lost his sense of time, said: "They really went over me yesterday." A man who saw me being brought down, through a crack in his cell window, later told me that I moved like an automation, having to be turned every time I headed for a wall which apparently I was unable to see. Another reason for this is that I was in such a state that my head could not possibly conceive of another movement or direction than that which at each moment I was set upon. Whenever a prisoner who has been tortured is brought down, prisoners not in solitary confinement are ordered into their underground communal cell, so that they will not be able to see him. Such orders are shouted at all times of the night, and there rarely passes a night without them. On one night I personally counted eight such orders.

After I had been subjected to the "falanga" treatment, I was thrown into a solitary confinement cell, where I was kept for fifteen days. The cells used for this purpose in the Athens Security Police Headquarters measure 1,80 meters in length and something like 0,80 in width. There is neither light nor aeration and the prisoner has to provide himself with a blanket in order to lie on the filthy bare cement floor. These cells are full of bugs, which provide many a prisoner with a unique way to pass time: burning them up one by one with his matches. Many people pass quite a number of days under what is called "severe isolation." This consists of no nourishment, no water, no cigarettes, and no access to the toilet, and no blanket. I lived under this regime for forty-eight hours. One does not usually mind the lack of food, but the lack of water is excruciating, especially after torture which leaves one without an ounce of moisture in the body. I was fortunate enough, on the second morning, to fall on a guard who was either half-human or had not yet received his day's orders and allowed me to go to the toilet, where I managed to drink from the water pipe leading into the turkish toilet, my hands and my lips touching the excrements others like myself had left floating there. I had to make water on the very cement floor on which I could not stand, sit or lie down except by balancing myself on the only two parts of my body which were not raw with pain: my hip bone and my elbow. Naturally I was unable to sleep for four days, as soon as my exhaustion overcame me I lost that only humanly bearable balance and woke up immediately screaming. But the worst part of being held in the Athens Security Police Headquarters is not one's own pain or thirst or suffering. It is the sounds. It is the screams of people being tortured, the moans, sometimes the weeping of your neighbors, the orders for the people not in solitary confinement to go down, and more than everything else the agonizingly soft, slow, five-minute, four-meter, interminable voyage on all fours of a tortured man whose name you do not know and whose face you cannot see from his cell to the toilet and then the whole bowel-tearing thing all over again on his way back.

Political prisoners in Greece only start being human again when they are safe in prison. Andreas Lendakis when he came to Averoff prison was still trembling with that interior trembling which is the residue of torture, physical and moral. It took him several days to be human again. But prison does not always give safety. I saw Ioannis Stratis the day he was brought back to prison from the Dionysos camp, where he had been taken from Averoff prison. His face and one eye were still swollen and red. He too did not look human. Very few people do after they have undergone the treatment reserved to political prisoners in Greece.

This very small part of the truth which I have recounted, wishing to confine myself only to those things, tangible proof of which I have personally witnessed, is at least indicative of what I set out to make clear: that the use of torture in Greece is not incidental but systematic and carried to a scale as large as the smallness of the country can permit, according to a pre-conceived plan of which no-one of the people actually ruling the country can disclaim responsibility.

I most urgently request this assembly to consider that at the very time this is being written and will be read, people in Greece are undergoing similar or worse treatment. I most urgently request this assembly to break the complicity which silence upon such practices creates.

Y. Leloudas

P.S. I must ask for my name and those parts of the above document which are in brackets to be kept secret, as my identification could lead to reprisals.

After the trial, Yiannis Leloudas began to serve his sentence. On the 23rd of December, Colonel Papadopoulos announced an amnesty and mentioned Mikis Theodorakis by name. This amnesty turned out to be a hoax, but because the new Prime Minister had mentioned Theodorakis by name and because there was foreign pressure for the composer's release, he was amnestied. Leloudas was one of the handful also released. He rejoined his wife, who had been arrested when she brought her husband food at the *Asphalia*. She, however, had been released after the trial.

Once again he was eligible for military service. The navy rejected him as a "security risk" when he refused to sign a paper swearing to report to the authorities any "antinational" activities that came to his attention. He was sent to the army. The army refused him and sent him back to the navy. The navy doctors found the heart defect once again and deferred him for another year.

Though he was watched by the Security Police, he managed to escape from Greece in the spring of 1969. He and his wife now live in Paris where he is a representative of the Patriotic Front abroad. Behind his reserve and behind his intelligent face on which a smile always comes as a surprise, there is an enormous nervous tension revealed only by his nicotine-stained fingers from his daily four packs of cigarettes. It is not a time for poetry or Indian archeology; the poetry he has written has no relevance to the new reality. Now his world is politics, and he is no longer a man of the Right. In the first summer after the coup, he, like others, worked to bring Greece back to April 20. Now all agree this is neither possible nor desirable. Leloudas now sees the problems of Greece as much deeper; Greece is a country where fundamental changes must be made if real democracy is to put down roots, and these changes must actually occur so that there won't be a military coup every time the people vote for change.

STELIOS NESTOR—Lawyer

Salonika is the second largest city in Greece, but has a very different style of life from the capital. Some say it is simply a large village where people are friendly and everyone knows everyone else. Though it can't be true that everyone knows everyone else, it does seem true of the elite, the milieu of intellectuals and traditional families.

Stelios Nestor, a warm man with an intelligent face and a good sense of humor, belonged to the circle of leading young citizens of Salonika known for their learning and liberal views. Nestor was a lawyer at the Court of Appeals of Salonika and was assistant to the Chair of Civil Law at the University before he resigned in 1966. He was also a member of the Executive Committee of the international organization, World University Service, headquartered in Geneva, and General Secretary of its Greek Committee. His talented wife, Alki, is the daughter of a professor of folklore studies at the University of Salonika, and she did a much-acclaimed doctoral dissertation in the same field.

It was a shock not only for Salonika but for all of Greece when many of Nestor's circle were arrested and disappeared. On the sixth of November, 1968, six men were put on trial before five military judges in Salonika. They were Nestor; Sotirios Dedes, a law professor; a former right-wing candidate for Parliament; a business man; an English teacher at the University; and Pavlos Zannas, former director of the Salonika Film Festival and Salonika's International Fair. The Zannas family name has always been in the forefront of past Greek struggles for freedom; now it was "antinational." The defendants were charged with "having acted in concert to spread ideas which had as their purpose the overthrow of the existing social system," with the "aggravating circumstance that these subversive ideas were spread in the press." They were accused of forming the "antinational" organization, "Democratic Defense of Salonika," distributing tracts, and putting stickers on cars which read, "Democracy will win." Since it was well known that they were not communists, the prosecutor could only claim that they were willing to collaborate with communists, "which would have led to violence." The defendants said that they were the true patriots, that they were acting to restore democracy in Greece.

They did not denounce their tortures as they had been threatened
with reprisals against their families if they spoke. The prosecutor
demanded ten years for Nestor, as the chief. Nestor did get the
heaviest sentence—sixteen and a half years.

In the early morning of May 24th, 1968, agents of KYP
(the Greek equivalent of the CIA), dressed in civilian
clothes, arrested me after entering my house carrying revolvers. Certain of them took me to the Chief of KYP
while others took the keys of my office where, without
my presence or that of anyone else, they made a search,
taking from my files whatever they considered useful.
After a few minutes stay at the Headquarters, I was again
taken by car to the National Security Police of Salonika,
where I remained for about half an hour. From there KYP
agents took me over and when they had handcuffed me they
put me in a car and covered my head with a piece of
cloth. The car set off towards the east of town, took the
road to the airfield, turned at the Agricultural School crossroads and entered the camp near Sedes airfield. Although
my face was covered, I am able to determine the place
where they took me because of characteristic details of
the journey, such as certain turnings (turnings at the entrance to and exit from Kennedy Avenue, the turning at
the Agricultural School, the turning at Sedes) and certain
points with distinctive lighting which I could make out
through the cloth over my eyes (the orange colored
lights at Kennedy Avenue, strong lights after relatively
great darkness on the journey at the crossroads at the
Agricultural School). At the gate of the camp the guards
had a few words with my escort and allowed the car to
pass, a certain sign that the camp was not unaccustomed
to noctural visitors. When the car stopped I was taken, with
my face still covered, to the enclosed part of a room where
the cloth was removed. Before and during the whole journey my escort advised me to tell what I knew so that I
should not be tortured.

In the room I found myself in the presence of four or
five people. One of them, tall and heavily built, approached me and punched me hard in the stomach. At
that moment a short young man came in who, as I ascertained later, during my detention, was Captain Kourkoulakos, who served in the KYP. He warned me that, if I did
not speak, I should be responsible for whatever followed.

On my refusal to answer, they ordered me to take off my shoes and two of the men brought in a rifle. They put my legs, at the ankles, between the rifle and the strap. Then they lifted the rifle to such a height that I was hanging upside-down with my bare soles uppermost. The tall man then took a thin whip and began to beat my soles, while Captain Kourkoulakos at every blow asked me various questions about people and things. After the first phase of the beating they raised me upright and ordered me to stamp heavily on the cement floor which had been made wet before. After this stamping, my feet swelled. Then the hanging upside-down and the beating were repeated. This proceeding was repeated several times. Each time I lost consciousness a bucket of water was thrown over my face. When finally my feet had open wounds from the beating, they lifted me up, and, because I could not stand upright, they put me, half fainting, up against the wall while two men hit me on the face and pulled hair out of my moustache. I have no accurate idea of the duration of my torture. I remember, however, that at some moments when they had me hanging and were beating me with a whip, I felt severe pain in my chest and had intense difficulty in breathing. My torturers were then afraid that I would die and stopped. Because I was soaking wet they transferred me to a cell in the detention cells of the KYP where I stayed for the remaining forty-seven days of my examination. Next day, because I could not get up and my clothes were soaked with blood, they wrapped me up in a blanket and took me to the office of the KYP Major, Anastasios Papaconstantinou, where they questioned me. During the examination, the Director of KYP, Major Papaconstantinou, was present. Although he saw my condition, he expressed no surprise whatever. The following days they provided no medical help, although I complained to someone who visited me that I felt pain from the probable dislocation of toes of my left foot. On the contrary, I was compelled to go almost crawling for my bodily needs to a filthy lavatory, at the risk of infecting my wounds. As a result of this beating, the joint of the second toe of my left foot was dislocated.

However, besides the physical torture, I was also subjected to mental violence with the purpose of extracting confessions. Thus, a week after I was arrested, Papaconstantinou and Kourkoulakos threatened that if I did not

speak they would arrest my wife. Subsequently they gave
orders in my presence to some agent to arrest my wife and
bring her to the torture chamber to undergo the "falanga,"
i.e. the torture I myself had suffered.

I was also held for forty-seven days in a cell measuring
about three feet 3 inches by ten feet six inches. Then at the
end of the preliminary inquiries I was sent with five other
detainees to a basement cell of the Transport Branch of
Salonika for three and a half months. This cell was without
natural light and because there was not sufficient space, we
were compelled to spend twenty-one of the twenty-four
hours lying or sitting on the floor. Throughout the whole of
my imprisonment in the Transport Branch we were allowed
to go out for one and a half hours in the morning and one
and a half in the afternoon into a small, sunless courtyard.

I will not refer here to the omissions and irregularities
of the proceedings, which were an obvious violation of the
principles of legality and establish them clearly as invalid.
I declare, however, that I am willing to confirm from the
beginning, to explain and expound to any competent agent
of the Council of Europe all I report in this present
statement.

Nestor is now serving his sentence in Aegina prison. Both he and
Dedes were deprived of their political rights for ten years from the
expiration of their sentences, [Decision of Salonika Military Court
No. 181/13.II.68.] as well as being permanently disbarred. [Royal
Decree in Ephemeris Tis Kyverniseos (Official Gazette) 453/1968.]

In March of 1969 the Minister of Justice, Mr. Kiriakopoulos,
once a professor at Salonika, decided to visit the political prisoners
there. He first encountered Dedes, a former student and colleague,
and told him, "I really am terribly sorry my friend, that you should
be here."

Dedes replied, "And I am terribly sorry for you, Professor."

The Minister entered the courtyard of the prison. None of the
prisoners got to his feet. He approached Nestor and said how much
he admired Mrs. Nestor, who was the daughter of his old friend,
Prof. Kiriakides. Nestor responded, "At the university you taught
us constitutional law, and I have followed your teachings. But, for
three and a half months while you have been Minister of Justice,
Professor Kiriakopoulos, I've been kept in the dungeon of an army
transit camp, I've been tortured, and passed before a mockery of a
court-martial whose decision you, Mr. Minister, have affirmed with
your own signature." Kiriakopoulos turned pale and began to stam-

mer while the other prisoners started chanting, "Freedom! Democracy! This is free Greece. You have no place here." Quietly the Minister told Nestor to go with him to the prison governor's office to make any requests he wanted. Nestor refused, saying he had nothing to ask of him.

ANGHELOS PNEVMATIKOS—Army Officer

Anghelos Pnevmatikos and his brother Costas were career military officers. Anghelos was a major in the infantry and Costas a captain in the engineers. Like almost all Greek officers, they had strong right-wing royalist convictions. They were accused of belonging to a resistance organization in the army. Costas was arrested on the twenty-fifth of March, 1968, in the Macedonian town of Skydra. When Costas refused to talk during his torture, Major Theophiloyiannakos kept repeating, "Why do you and Anghelos protect that good-for-nothing bum of a king?"

> 22.3.68 I was arrested in Athens, and taken to the General Security (Asphalia).
>
> 24.3.68 I was transferred from the Security to regimental prison (EAT/ESA). It was dark, the mattress hardly fit in the narrow cell, and the interrogators worked in shifts.
>
> 25-26.3.68 Theophiloyannokos slapped me twice in front of Papageorghiou and Madame Katina.
>
> 2.4.68 They took my first deposition.
>
> 3.4.68 At noon, I was led to K.E.S.A. (Greek Military Police Center). An old stable, it was transformed into a jail. There was the smell of urine everywhere. In the cell there was a bed frame and three planks, no mattress, and no blanket. It was very cold. A soldier brought food, leaving it on the ground in a tin can, without a spoon. Everything was disgustingly filthy. He put the bread on the ground in the filth, and to one side there was a pail full of garbage and human excrement. No sooner had he brought the food

which I couldn't bring myself to eat, than the noise of a
Harley motorcycle started up right outside my ground floor
window. For three hours I was tyrannized by this infernal
noise. This was repeated several times. Nobody came to see
me until the evening when a soldier came and left food in
the same way as he had before. All night long they banged
on the metal doors and the bars, and at the same time my
only light blinked constantly on and off. I stayed this way
until Saturday evening April 6. Then the Commandant,
Major Papageorghiou paid me a visit. He spoke in a
threatening tone, "Now Mister Big Deal, why don't you
confess? If you don't, you'll see what will happen to you."

He made me get in a jeep with two soldiers of the
military police, and they brought me to Dionysos where
the 505th Battalion is located. The commander is Yiannis
Manouskakis. They took me directly to the detention cells,
at the far end of the military camp, at the foot of Mount
Pendeli near some trees. It was a low building with six
cells, each measuring one meter by two meters thirty and
two meters high. The building was covered with sheet metal,
the doors were made of wood and there were no windows.
There was no natural light, nor electric light, there was a
bed, a mattress, but no blanket. I had hardly been shut in
when officers visited me one by one, dressed in shirts or
sweaters or just undershirts. They all carried pistols at their
belts. Some of them wore civilian clothes and military boots,
I suppose so I wouldn't learn their rank and identity. They
had a powerful electric light which they flashed in my eyes
when they asked me various questions.

Finally one came and ordered me to take off my clothes
and my shoes. I refused to take off my pants, and told
them an officer did not strip this way, and if they wanted
to take them off they would have to do it by force. He
went away. (Because I was freezing from the cold I demanded to see a doctor for my heart and chest. It was on
his advice that they later gave back my clothes and I was
allowed to wear a cotton undershirt and my shirt.)

A dozen of them gathered outside my door and started
making a tremendous racket, beating with metal rods and
sticks on the sheet metal. They continued this for a long
time, taking only short breaks of three to five minutes,
during which an officer came in and demanded that I confess, because if I didn't I would be tortured.

They ordered me again to take off my clothes. I refused. They started beating me with a club but I managed to grab it. Then they brought wild dogs that were held on chains and they goaded them on, pushing them into the cell to bite me, all the time shouting, "Bulgarian traitor! Wretch! Communist! Fairy! You're going to die tonight! Cross yourself!" Shortly thereafter Candidate Officer Sideropoulos grabbed me by the throat shouting, "Just like the Communists killed my father, I'm going to kill you, cut your throat with a piece of jagged metal!" All these insults, threats and noises were made by a group of officers who were just outside my cell. These scenes lasted until three in the morning when I heard someone who said, "He's not giving in. Me, I'm leaving, but you keep it up." He added something in a low voice, but I couldn't make it out. I heard a jeep drive off, it was probably Papageorghiou and Basil Ioannides who were leaving. (This last one belongs to the G-2 of the General Staff of the 505th.)

This situation lasted until morning, when the Commander of the Third Company came to visit me. He told me his name, though not his rank, and he wasn't wearing any insignia. He demanded that I confess. Toward eleven o'clock in the morning I was called to the office of the Deputy Commander of the 505th. Also there was Major Basilis Ioannides as well as the commander of the Third Company. They offered me a coffee. They were all in uniform and they demanded that I confess. They said I should reflect on what awaited me if I didn't. Since I refused I was once again sent back to my cell where every half-hour there was the noise of the sheet metal, the attacks of the dogs and the visits of the candidate officers. This went on without any let-up until the afternoon of Monday, April 8, 1968. It was then that I was called to the office of the Commander of the 505th, Yiannis Manouskakis.

Up to this point I hadn't eaten or drunk water since the third of April. He offered me some french-fried potatoes in his office and said that everything that had gone on had happened without his knowledge and "it wouldn't be repeated."

Actually nothing did happen Monday evening, but it all began again on Tuesday the 9th of April.

9.4.68 Before they began to beat me again, Major Koutras visited me and asked me to confess, promised me that if

I did, he would free my brother Costas and the other prisoners. I refused.

Before I underwent *falanga,* Major Ioannides used the method of burial on me. "Angelos," he said, "you better confess, because you will regret it if you don't." Behind the prison is a trench in which they put individuals and cover them with sand, leaving only the head unburied. The time of burial depends on the resistance of the victim. I cannot say how long I was buried there, because the anguish, the nervous strain and the constant questions shouted by people working in rotation gave false impressions of time. Those that collaborated with Ioannides in this were the Officer Candidate Visanyaris and Sideropoulos. The Battalion doctor supervised the operation from the medical standpoint.

Tuesday evening an Officer Candidate arrived who began to beat me with karate punches on the back of the neck and in the stomach. I hit back until a second one came and grabbed me by the thumb of my left hand, twisting it, while the two continued to beat me without pity until the next morning.

Then I was taken to the office of Ioannides. He was there along with the Deputy Commander and the Commander of the Third Company. Again I refused to talk and they led me back to my cell where I was beaten until evening. At 20 hours they took me again to the office of the head of the 505th where were Ioannides, the commander of the Third Company and a captain. They began to beat me with their fists, and finally threw me into the office of the Deputy Commander. In the office there was a camp bed without a mattress. Some of the officers watched me while the others held me down. The whole operation was directed by Ioannides. They hit me on the soles of the feet. Then they took me to the office where again I refused to talk. I was taken back for more and had three or four more falanga sessions until I passed out on the floor. They picked me up, putting me in an armchair while they called a doctor. He ordered me moved to the infirmary where the doctor took care of me until Thursday noon. It must pointed out that I had not eaten since the fifth of April.

15.4.68 They transferred me from the 505th to the EAT/ESA.

20.4.68 I was moved to the K.E.S.A. in the same cell as

before. They brought me a table and a chair and three days later, a mattress. During all this time, I had seen no one of my family and I didn't have permission to take a shower or even wash until the fourth of May. Major Theophiloyannakos threatened me that if I didn't speak, he would bring my brother's sons and tell them that their father was staying in prison because that was what I wanted. At the ESA/SA Lt. Col. Ioannides visited me and repeated the same things.

31.5.68 I was transferred to Salonika, at first to the 616th Infantry Battalion and after on 1.6.68 to the Second Commissariat of Police, Kalamarias, where I was put in solitary confinement.

Anghelos Pnevmatikos

Anghelos Pnevmatikos and Costas were finally brought before a court-martial. Despite the fact that they testified, they were tortured, given prison terms, and committed to Coridallos Prison of Piraeus.

Anghelos did not let the matter rest there. He brought a suit against Prime Minister Papadopoulos as being responsible for his torture. On April 19, 1969, it was Anghelos who was brought to trial for "insulting the Prime Minister." This trial was held behind closed doors as the court-martial was afraid he would not only speak about his torture but also about the plotting in the army before April 21, 1969. Despite the fact that the regime announced in the summer that courts-martial were to be restricted, the court refused to accept the objection that under the law courts-martial did not have jurisdiction over slander. When the accused demanded that his brother Costas appear as a necessary witness a document was produced from the director of the prison saying he could not appear as he was classified as a person too dangerous for escaping. Anghelos in court pointed to one of the military judges and asked how could he get a fair trial when that judge had been present during his torture. Anghelos was found guilty and sentenced to five years. What constitutes a grave offense in Greece can be seen from the fact that on the same day before another court-martial a former army captain was found guilty of spying for Yugoslavia and given a one year suspended sentence. [*International Herald Tribune,* Nov. 20, 1969.]

PETROS VLASSIS—Student

Petros Vlassis comes from the island of Corfu, "the Emerald of the Ionian Sea." Vlassis is short and stocky, with the bluish eyes of a northern Greek; his movements and speech have the direct quality of the villager. His village, Lefkimi, on the southern tip of the island, was built back from the sea in such a way as to be protected from the Barbary pirates of the last century. His father is a tailor, and by the standards of Lefkimi the family is neither rich nor poor. Their wealth is measured in Greek fashion: forty olive trees, three *stremata* (two-thirds of an acre) of vineyards, one *strema* of oranges, potatoes, and tomatoes. The mother does all the work of the fields, while the father, handicapped by a chronic eczema, does what little tailoring work there is available. Politically the family tradition is that of Venizelos, of republicanism. During the occupation the father helped the partisans in the village and was arrested by the Italians. Though the father is a man of Center Union convictions and voted for Papandreou, the son says that the police have a file on him as a communist because he did not vote in the plebiscite for the king in 1946.

Petros, the oldest of three children, proved to be an intelligent boy, doing well in primary school with little studying. His father considered him disobedient, but the more he beat his son, the more his son disobeyed. By high school Petros was seldom at home; he was always off with his friends, hunting birds with a slingshot or spearfishing in the sea. Though he rarely studied and had to repeat a school year, he worried over fundamental questions of man and society. He read a book on the philosophy of materialism thirteen times and sought out any priest who would discuss the question of God's existence. During the elections of 1961 he first came to the attention of the local police who noticed that he was associating with "leftists." He finished high school in June of 1962 and tried to enter the army immediately to discharge his military obligation, but he was told there were no places. His father did not have enough money to send him to the university, but that was what Petros wanted, and with twenty dollars he set off for Athens on the path that would lead him six years later to the *terraza* of Bouboulinas Street.

Through a tailor who had once apprenticed to his father, he found a place to live—a basement room with six others, which cost them each two dollars a month. He found a job. A year later he entered the university in the Faculty of Economics and Commerce. He continued to work and held many jobs during these years— waiter, bookbinder, errand boy, doorman, salesman.

On May 23, 1963, a left-wing deputy, George Lambrakis, was murdered by the police in Salonika, where he had gone to preside over a pacifist meeting. (This political murder has been dramatized for a world audience by the French movie, Z.) The day after his death an organization was founded—the Grigoris Lambrakis Democratic Youth Movement. Petros joined this organization and found there the idealism which he had not found in Christian youth organizations. The movement caught the imagination of much of Greek youth and at one time claimed a membership of 80,000. In time, the left-wing party, EDA, infiltrated the directorship and gained control over the organization. Their own youth movement was then merged with the Lambrakis movement.

The summer of 1965 brought the "king's coup" against George Papandreou, and there were demonstrations in the streets. One student was killed that summer. A new organization bearing his name, Petroulis, was founded, and it held that the EDA was as bourgeois as the parties of the right and that the youth had to look for something new and revolutionary. Petros came back from his village for the fall semester and didn't know which group to join. Finally he stayed with the Lambrakis and worked all that year to gain back those that had been lost to the Petroulis organization, now a bitter foe of the Lambrakides.

In May of 1966 Petros was arrested for the first time. Coming out of the Lambrakis headquarters, he was stopped by a plain-clothesman who asked to see his identity card. Petros pulled out his wallet and with it a wad of receipts for money he had collected for the organization. He was taken to the police station and charged with collecting funds without the necessary permit. He spent a night in detention, then he was tried and sentenced to three months. Filing an appeal rather than taking a suspended sentence, he was released and later won his appeal. Throughout this experience he was correctly treated. The news reached Corfu in the newspapers. His family was very upset by his political activity; his mother was "nearly crazy."

It was only natural that after the coup the Security Police would be watching Petros as a probable resister. Just as it was natural that he would join the student resistance organization, Rigas Ferraios. Founded in December of 1967, it was named after Greece's poet of independence and attracted students of all political positions. Though it stood for the overthrow of the military regime and the establishment of democracy, its activities were nonviolent. The members published a mimeographed broadsheet, *Thourios,* wrote slogans on walls, and once planted a tape recorder in a meeting of the Philosophy Faculty which played out, "Long live democracy, long live Rigas Ferraios!"

On April 21, 1967, I was a member of "Lambrakis Democratic Youth." Because of this political position of mine, I was arrested on May 8, 1967, in the corridor of my school by Police Officer Vlassios Karathanassis, who belongs to the "cultural" branch of the Security Police and is responsible for the School of Economics and Commerce. Under the threat of his revolver I was led to the General Security Police Headquarters of Athens at Bouboulinas Street and taken to the office of Police Captain Karapanayiotis.

There I was subjected to both kind words and threats such as, "We are going to throw you out of the window and nothing will be reported to anyone." They "persuaded" me to write a curriculum vitae in exchange for being released. I filled in ten to twelve big pages starting from the day I was born to the present moment. At five o'clock in the afternoon I still had not finished. I then passed into the hands of Police Lieutenant Vassilios Gravaritis.

Sitting in an office opposite that of Karapanayiotis and surrounded by ten policemen, I was told by Gravaritis, although I had already finished the curriculum vitae, to declare my obedience to the junta and to renounce my past by condemning my ideas, my friends and in general all the Greeks who do not submit. My refusal to do so was the beginning of my ordeal.

Gravaritis, Karathanassis, Christakis, Logothetis, Papangelis and the others started by slapping, punching and kicking me. They used truncheons, rods, rulers and a whip. When the rods or the rulers broke, they used the sharp pieces for piercing me. When I was thrown to the floor, I tried to get under the desk to protect myself. I'll never forget when Policeman Papangelis threw a chair at me. It missed, hitting the wall and smashing into pieces. Those ten continued beating me until ten o'clock at night without stopping at all. Once during this period I heard the voice of Karathanassis saying, "Let's throw him out of the window!"

They all agreed, "the sooner the better!" Gravaritis and Karathanassis held me by the armpits and two others by my feet. They lifted me to the height of a window which opened out onto a small interior courtyard. They pushed me out, and I found myself hanging in a void held only under the arms by Gravaritis and Karathanassis and by a third policeman who grasped the back of my shirt. Very short was the time I remained in that position, but very long was my agony facing death under my feet.

At about ten o'clock that night I was thrown into underground cell number seven. When, in a way, I found my senses and could stand up, I saw that the small windows on my door didn't close well. Through this hold I managed to see some of my co-detainees. I saw the Athens Secretary of EDA, Manoussos, who was horribly beaten. His face and especially the hollows of his eyes were completely black. I also saw my fellow student, Petros Kaparelis, the actor, Manos Katrakis, Mrs. Iliou, and many others I didn't know. I also saw an old paralytic who was transferred from his cell to the toilet and back by more than two persons.

Around midnight one of my fellow detainees gave me something to eat. I hadn't even swallowed the first bite when everything grew dark in front of me. I fainted. More than an hour passed before I regained my senses.

The next day the traffic was heavy in the underground cells at Bouboulinas Street. Most of the detainees were transferred to Yaros. Others took their place, and then they in their turn increased the population of the rocky islands of the Aegean Sea.

That day I was only called twice to the office of Gravaritis. After some punching and kicking I was sent back to cell number eleven.

On the third day after my arrest at about six o'clock in the evening I was taken to Karapanayiotis's office. There I found myself facing some close relatives of mine. Under that psychological pressure I was forced to sign the dirty paper. I was immediately "released" with the obligation to report to the Security Police twice a week.

My relatives were crying as we left the Security Police building. At home I took off my clothes. I saw myself and my relatives saw me. What? A body black from head to toe. They exclaimed, "My boy, even the Germans didn't behave like that. *Anathema, anathema!*"

Besides my relatives, there are about thirty other people who have seen my blackened body.

At the beginning of my enslaved freedom I reported to the Security Police twice a week, later on only once, and finally every fortnight.

During my "visits" there I saw and heard the following: I saw Karathanassis transferring an acquaintance of mine from the underground area to the upstairs. He was in a very bad condition, extremely weak and pale, and unable to stand on his own feet, he was leaning on Karathanassis in order to walk. His expression was empty and he gave the impression not of a man but a shadow.

Another time as I was entering the building I heard a woman screaming. As I climbed the stairs the screams grew louder and louder. At the end of the fourth stairs I met a policeman. He asked me what my name was and why I was there. He told me to go away immediately and he himself would mark me present in the book. The screams were terrible, they were coming from the terrace. I could not stand up, my legs would not support me. I leaned against the wall so as not to fall down. The screams were so expressive. Never in my life had I heard such howlings, howlings of pain.

Another time I saw Gravaritis, Voyatzis and others punching an old man while he was being loaded into a car to be transferred to the ship for the islands of the Aegean. Among them were Greek Resistance fighters against the Germans such as Stergios Mavromatis and Yiannis Palavos.

A year later on May 27, 1968, at eight o'clock in the morning I stepped down from the bus at the corner of Patriarchou Ioakim Street and Loukianou Street. Like every morning I was on my way to my job. However, Karathanassis and another Security Policeman appeared and arrested me. They pinned my arms behind me, handcuffed me, and started to beat me. This was right in Kolonaki Square. The people stood there and watched. Blood started coming from my mouth and nose. They didn't stop, but kept on beating me behind a newspaper kiosk until a police car came. I was shoved in and still the beating didn't stop. Finally the police driver protested because my blood was dirtying the upholstery of the car.

We arrived at the General Security Police Headquarters at Bouboulinas Street, and I was brought before Gravaritis. With five or six other policemen, he led me up to the terrace. On entering the room I faced a bench and a thick rope, behind the bench pieces of wood were strewn about the floor. To the right there were four or five showers and a water heater. About one or two meters from the water heater there is a door.

As soon as I entered the room, they started undressing me. They took off everything except my shoes. They made me lie on the bench. Gravaritis started tying me down while Karathanassis got up on me and stepped on me from me feet to my chest in order to make my body fit perfectly to the bench.

After I was securely fastened from the ankles to the neck, the torment of *falanga* began. They beat my feet with rough rods which were about one meter long and three centimeters wide. Two men alternately beat me at a fixed rhythm. A third man kept a dirty cloth over my mouth so that my screams could not be heard.

I did not feel my feet at all. I fainted. They untied me, threw water over me, and I came back to my senses. When I came to, I realized I was surrounded by ten policemen who were holding sticks and ropes. They were all hitting me and making me run so that my numb feet would regain sensation.

They succeeded in their purpose and then tied me again on the bench. While the torment of *falanga* was repeated, Gravaritis was punching me in the stomach, the abdomen and other parts of my body.

I fainted again. Again they untied me, threw water on me and formed a circle around me to beat me. And again I was tied to the bench for another round of *falanga*. During *falanga* they also beat the upper part of my feet. As a result of this my big toe nails later dropped off.

At this point the *falanga* torment was finishing and the torment of Gravaritis was to start.

Tied on the bench and with the dirty cloth over my mouth, I was beaten by Police Lieutenant Gravaritis on the bones. Using a thick piece of wood he started on the ankles, then hit the shin bones and the knees. After he finished with the legs he worked on arms and hands. Then he beat me on the testicles and tore me trying to push the wood up my rectum. That ordeal together with the beatings on the upper part of my fingers, on the elbows and on the bones generally, was the most horrible of all. I could not move my legs. Gravaritis himself put wet pieces of cloth on my legs to try to bring them back to life.

When I reached the point of being able to sit up, all the old torturers, except one, left. Five or six young men between the ages of twenty and twenty-five then appeared with police officer Kalyvas. Kalyvas slapped and punched me. The young torturers glared at me like tigers. Gravaritis then appeared together with an Army captain. He threatened me, saying that the moment had come for me to be transferred to Dionysos Camp for further interrogations.

After I had in a way found my senses, I was held up by two policemen and in this way taken down to Kalyvas's office. There my deposition was to be taken, and I was to confront Pavlos Klavdianos, who was supposed to have spoken against me.

A few minutes later Pavlos was brought to the office without knowing why. I was made to turn around and Pavlos was made to back toward me. After being threatened and pressured and after many hesitations, he said, "I gave to Vlassis the newspaper 'Thourios' of Rigas Fereos." However when he turned around and our eyes met, he said, "I lied. You forced me to lie."

After that statement they took him away. They took away a different person than the one I had known. His eyes were sunk deep in their sockets. His skin stuck on his bones. His color was that of a dead man. He was hardly able to walk; the marks of torture were clearly visible on the uncovered parts of his body. He looked like those men from the concentration camps of Hitler which we sometimes see at the movies.

Then at about two-thirty in the morning they threw me into underground cell five. My name was "five" from that day on until I was released on Saturday, June 15, 1968. During those twenty days I was often taken to Kalyvas's office for interrogation. Police Captain Karapanayiotis proposed to give me 2000 drachmas as a starting salary if I would become his agent. In other words he was asking me to become a member of a resistance organization for the sole purpose of giving him the names of the patriots. It is hard to express one's feelings when you realize your conscience, your human values, and you as a human being, have been torn apart.

Karapanayiotis, together with Police Lieutenant Gravaritis, told me the following: "The International Red Cross came to verify tortures. We are not dopes. We took them to the terrace, but they saw nothing, because it all had been changed into nicely arranged storerooms. Surely you must realize that we are the best police in the world."

The first three days I had no food. The Security Police doesn't give any and my relatives did not know where I was.

During those twenty days in spite of the fact that I was in solitary confinement, I saw many people, some of whom I knew and others I didn't. Most of them had been beaten. Some of the students I knew who showed clearly the marks of torture were: Pavlos Klavdianos, Athanassios Athanassiou, Sotirios Anastasiasdis, Andreas Savakis, Constantine Savakis. Also there was Yiannis Petropoulos, who is not a student but who like all the others was yellowed, thin and had great difficulty walking. There also was Yiannadakis and many others whose names I can't say as they are not free and just mentioning their names would be enough for them to visit the terrace again.

In the underground cells not only were there those people who were being accused but also those with no accusations who were to be sent to the islands. One of these, Zoi Xenaki, a student at my school, spent five months in a cell with two other women and then finally was transferred to Yaros on June 13, 1968.

For being let free I signed another declaration. Among many other statements was the following: "Any future trial and conviction of mine will be just, and I will not have the right to appeal or denounce it."

On June 22, 1968, I met in Athens Mr. Van der Stoel and the British M.P., Mr. Paul Rose, to whom I described my case and showed the marks of torture still on me.

On January 23, 1969, I was inducted into the army and was with the 6th Infantry Corps stationed in Corinth. A few days after I reported, I was called to A2 (Army Intelligence). There I was beaten. The Captain of A2, threatening me with torture and court martial, ordered me to fill in a curriculum vitae and to sign a declaration of obedience to the military regime as well as to renounce and condemn my past, my ideas, and my friends.

After I signed, I left. Within a week I was called in again to define my position toward the following, The Greek Communist Part (K.K.E.), the agreement between

Andreas Papandreou and Antonis Brillakis, the 21st of
April, 1967, and the new constitution.

After doing all of this, a new psychological war was
started against me. The sub-lieutenant of the 7th Company, Alexander Viliotis, organized a whole network of
soldiers to spy on me. He started to humiliate me, challenge
and insult me. He was punishing me for no reason and
along with the sub-lieutenant Panayiotis Kyriakakis, who
was carrying out the duties of a captain, told me, "In order
to show you are an honest man and not a woman, you
must commit suicide."

To give an example of the psychological violence which
is practised in the army, the Commander of the 3rd Company, Captain Dionyssios Dertinopoulos, ordered his officers and non-commissioned officers to bring every day two
or three soldiers who were against the junta and punish
them, as was his power, with five days imprisonment. I
knew one person who served more time imprisoned than in
the army.

Under these conditions of constant humiliation and blackmail, I thought that my duty to my country was not to
serve the military regime, the pronounced enemy of myself, my friends and generally of all Greek people, but to
tell the truth to the sub-commission of Human Rights.

For these reasons I abandoned my beloved country and
the fascist army, believing that it is in this way that I am
serving the interests of Greece.

The *Asphalia* told Petros that he was the seventieth and last
person to be arrested in the *Rigas Ferraios* affair. Petros says that
he was the least tortured. This does not mean that he has suffered
the least. For he is a man who has signed. He has renounced his
beliefs and his friends. For other Greeks, no matter how much
they sympathize with what he had to go through, he is a fallen
man. As Petros says, "When you fall into the hands of the
Asphalia, they break you either physically or morally."

In this environment of torture and humiliation, Petros signed his
allegiance to the "National Revolutionary Government" and he was
freed. His friend Pavlos Klavdianos and others refused to sign. [The
deposition of Klavdianos, aged 23, submitted to the Human Rights
Commission gives an example of what happened to one who refused
to cooperate:

KLAVDIANOS, Pavlos, aged 23, student at the School

of Economic and Commercial studies. I was arrested on February 29, 1968, by policeman Karathanasis; taken to the General Security Headquarters of Athens; beaten up on the way. At the office of police officer Kalyvas, Ioannis, I was beaten up by Kalyvas, Karapanagiotis, Karathanasis, and others. They used sticks, rubber straps and wires. They tied and pulled my genitals with a string. Then I was taken to the roof where there is a shed. They tied me on a table and tortured me beating the soles of my feet with a stick, the *falanga*. At the same time they were hitting me on the thighs, chest and the whole body. They ordered me to walk around the table while fifteen policemen were hitting me. Then they put me on the table again and continued the *falanga*. The torture went on the whole night. In the morning they took me to cell 20, where I was kept in solitary confinement. On March 7, 1968, I was summoned for interrogation. There Kalyvas, Karathanasis and Kravaritis beat me and led me to the shed on the roof. The *falanga* was repeated and followed by beatings on my genitals. The same day I was transferred to the camp of the 505 Marine Battalion at Dionysos. Immediately I was submitted to the *falanga;* the palm of my right hand was burnt with a lit cigarette. Transferred to the detention room, I remained there for 38 days and was submitted to the *falanga* by Major Boufas, Konstantinos, Major A2 (Army Intelligence Service) Ioannidis, Vassilios, and other cadets and petty officers. Lieutenant Spyropoulos put electric wires on my forehead and neck and connected them with an electric source. That happened twice. Then I was stripped naked in the rain and was obliged to run in the courtyard of the headquarters in front of the whole battalion. I was prevented from sleeping because the guard made some continuous noise on purpose. Some days later they told me to lie on the floor of the room and they put a water can over my head and let drops of water fall on my forehead with the result that I suffered acute headaches. They hung me by the hands and hit me in the stomach. My shoulders were dislocated. They hung me up holding me by the ears. During the night they brought big dogs into the cell and left them there. By order of the commandant, Manoussakakis, Ioannis, two soldiers and a sergeant of ESA (military police) tried to rape me. Because I resisted their efforts they stopped giving me food and water. Manoussakakis hit me

with his revolver at his office and pretended he was going
to kill me.

On April 13 or 14 I was transferred back to Security in
Athens at Bouboulinas where I was beaten once at the
office with a whip and once with sticks under the soles of
my feet while I was held seated in a chair. My detention
both at General Security and Dionysos lasted three months.
For many days I was refused food and water. I am still
feeling pains on the soles of my feet and in the stomach.
Security notified my family of my arrest 25 days after the
event, though my family had repeatedly asked about me at
Security Headquarters, specifically police officer Karapanagiotis. The Athens Special Military Court sentenced me
on November 20, 1968, to twenty-one (21) years of
imprisonment.

For refusing to sign, Pavlos Klavdianos and others were systematically tortured for long periods of time at Dionysos and Bouboulinas.
On November 20, 1968, sixteen students of *Rigas Ferraios* were
brought before a military court. With one exception they bravely
denounced their tortures and defended their actions and beliefs. For
being a member of the organization and passing on a copy of
"Thourios," Klavdianos received twenty-one years in prison. Petros
was free. But inside himself he was not free. He felt so inferior to
Klavdianos and the others, his shame was destroying him. Perhaps
this explains why he took the desperate step of deserting from the
army to escape to testify before the European Human Rights Commission. He feels by this act he has atoned in part for his "cow-
ardice," but he wonders, "What are they in prison thinking of me
now? If tomorrow we are all free, will they put their arms around
me? "

DOCUMENTS

I. AMNESTY INTERNATIONAL

Amnesty International is a "humanitarian organization without any religious or political affiliation" founded to help "prisoners of conscience" all over the world. "Prisoners of conscience" are defined as those who have neither practiced nor advocated violence but are imprisoned for their political or religious beliefs. Amnesty bases its work on Articles 18 and 19 of the Universal Declaration of Human Rights. [The Universal Declaration was proclaimed at the United Nations on December 10, 1948. Article 18: Everyone has the right to freedom of thought, conscience and religion; this right includes freedom to change his religion or belief, and freedom, either alone or in community with others and in public or private, to manifest his religion or belief in teaching, practice, worship and observance.

Article 19: Everyone has the right to freedom of opinion and expression; this right includes freedom to hold opinions without interference and to seek, receive and impart information and ideas through any media and regardless of frontiers.]

Amnesty International was started in 1961, the brainchild of an English barrister, Peter Benenson. His experience with political prisoners in many lands made him aware of the great need to do something about the thousands of innocent men and women being persecuted for their beliefs. Too often such people were locked away, totally forgotten. Benenson set up a bureau to collect information on cases, publicize them, and organize practical help. Within a month he had over a thousand offers of support. Within two months representatives from five countries had established the beginnings of an international network of groups willing to help.

The basic unit of Amnesty is the working group. A group of three to ten people "adopts" one prisoner from each power bloc, the West, the East and the Third World. The groups try to mobilize public opinion, write letters to the competent authorities, to do, in short, what they can to obtain the release of their adopted prisoner and give concrete help to the prisoner's family. Today there are nineteen National Sections, more than 650 groups, and an active membership of over four thousand. England, Sweden, and Germany have the largest National Sections.

The International Secretariat is located in London. It is here that information is centralized and contact with the National Sections and groups coordinated. By searching through the press and other sources, Amnesty learns of cases, investigates them, and sends them out for adoption.

Apart from the basic activities done by the groups, the Secretariat sends delegates to different countries when it is believed that an investigation on the spot would be of particular value. Before the coup d'etat in Greece, Amnesty had six prisoners of conscience whom it considered political and a larger number of Jehovah's Witnesses imprisoned for refusal to do military service. The coup d'etat brought a problem of new and grave dimensions. After the coup there were 6,337 deported by administrative decision alone. (There were 2,815 in 1950, that is during the Civil War. By 1963 there were none.) Greece appeared a suitable place for a special Amnesty effort, and two lawyers, the author and Anthony Marreco, were sent there at the end of December, 1967. We wrote the following report.

Situation in Greece

Report by Amnesty International

1. Amnesty International (which enjoys Consultative Status Category I with the Council of Europe) sent a Delegation to Greece on December 30, 1967, for the purpose of (a) investigating the extent and implementation of the amnesty for political prisoners announced on December 22,

and (b) obtaining information concerning the economic and other conditions of dependents of political prisoners not released under the amnesty. Mr. Antony Marreco, a member of the English Bar, and Mr. James Becket, a member of the American Bar, remained in Greece until January 26, 1968.

2. The Delegation presented its Order of Mission to the Ministry of Foreign Affairs and requested the following facilities:

i) A list of the political prisoners detained with brief particulars of the charges to be preferred against them;

ii) Permission to attend as observers and report upon the hearings of the Judicial Committees which, as announced by the Minister of Justice, are to review the cases of all political prisoners;

iii) Permission to accompany the Representative of the International Red Cross to the prison establishments on the islands of Leros and Yaros;

iv) Meetings with officials of the Ministries of Justice and Public Order as might be appropriate.

Meetings took place at the Ministry of Foreign Affairs on January 2, 4, 10 and 24; while the officials were courteous, none of the above facilities have so far been granted.

3. The Delegation, however, spent four weeks taking statements from prisoners who had been released and from relatives of prisoners still in detention. As a result of the four-week investigation the Delegation reports as follows:

(a) The Ministry of Justice has announced that 284 prisoners have been released under Constitutional Act No. 16 of December 23, and Law No. 228 of December 26 (the Christmas Amnesty). Some of these were not in fact released, but simply transferred under Law No. 509 to the islands, and in any case the declared amnesty did not apply to those not yet charged with any crime. The approximate numbers of prisoners detained without trial by the Greek Government at the end of January are as follows:

LEROS	Laki	1,475	
	Partheni	500	
YAROS		802	(including 240 women)
		2,777	

In addition there are numerous prisoners held without trial in prisons and police stations throughout Greece. It is believed that of those detained some 500 may have been active or potentially active communists. The remainder cannot be described as "communists" in any accepted European sense of the word, and large numbers of them are old and infirm, having been arrested on security files prepared in many cases twenty years ago. It seems a feature of the present regime that the Government treats such persons as expendable outcasts to be deprived of all political rights.

The Delegation has assembled the names, addresses and particulars of about eight hundred of those detained on Leros and Yaros; the prisoners come from all walks of life and include parliamentarians, professional people, intellectuals and artists. Many remain in prison only because they refuse to sign the Declaration of Loyalty (see Appendix A, which speaks for itself).

(b) The Delegation found that the relatives of prisoners have been subject to Government persecution. Children of the prisoners are excluded from entering University. Friends have been arrested for giving money to needy families. Relatives have lost their jobs. The police pay frequent harassing visits to the families of prisoners at all hours of the day and night.

4. The Delegation investigated allegations that the regime is practising the infliction of pain as an aid to interrogation. (For details of the nature and method of torture used, see Appendix B.) Despite the atmosphere of fear, especially among those who have been released and who can report how they have been tortured, and despite the extreme difficulties and time necessary in making contact, 16 people testified to the Delegation that they had been tortured. The Delegation also obtained and checked the names of 32 other persons who are in prison and who are alleged to have been tortured. On the basis of firsthand evidence and oral testimony, on the basis of scars on the bodies of those tortured, and on the basis of testimony of professional people and relatives, the Delegation can objectively state that torture is deliberately and officially used and was convinced that the use of torture is a widespread practice against Greek citizens suspected of active opposition to the Government. The Delegation in its month-long investigation was only able to investigate the situation in the Athens area. For a Greek outside the capital, contact with a foreigner is too dangerous to be risked. Though the Delegation heard reports of torture and other degrading treatment in the provinces, it was second-hand evidence and therefore nothing in this report is based on such allegations. However, there is no doubt that formal evidence can be taken on commission if the Greek Government will agree to a procedure to guarantee the future safety of witnesses.

January 27, 1968
Turnagain Lane
Farringdon Street
London, E. C. 4.

Appendix B—Torture

The following account presents in summary form the evidence the Amnesty International Delegation took from the 16 people they saw who reported that they had been tortured, and from the 32 people still in prison about whose cases they received secondhand evidence which they found convincing because it was in many cases corroborated.

Organizations, Places and Persons Engaged in Torture

Torture as a deliberate practice is carried out by the Security Police (Asphalia) and the Military Police (Ethniki Stratiotiki Astinomia). The Delegation heard firsthand evidence that the army and the gendarmerie also carried out torture, but it was difficult to determine if these were isolated cases or standard procedure.

Those whose names are most frequently mentioned as directing and carrying out torture are: Inspector Lambrou, the Director of the Security Police Headquarters in Athens at Bouboulinas Street, and the following officers—Mallios, Babalis, Karapanayiotis, Kravaritis, Spanos, Yannicopoulos, all of the same office; Major Theophiloyaiannakos of the Military Police located at the Dionysos Camp outside Athens. Others mentioned frequently were Zagouras at Dionysos, Lt. Kapoglou, Director of Asphalia at Aigeleo, and Kouvas of the Asphalia in Pircus.

The places where the most serious torture was reported in the Athens area are the Bouboulinas Asphalia, Military Hospital 401, and the Dionysos camp.

Techniques of Torture

A. *Physical Torture*

1. The standard initial torture reported from every Asphalia station is the so-called *falanga*. The prisoner is tied to a bench and the soles of his feet are beaten with a stick or pipe. Between beatings the prisoner is usually made to run around the bench under a heavy rain of blows. We examined the feet of a person who suffered this treatment four months before and his sole was covered with thick scar tissue. One prisoner now in Averoff prison had his foot broken under this torture. As he went without medical attention, the bones have not set properly and he is crippled. The next step in this method is to strike the prisoner on the sternum. Prisoners vomiting blood from the lungs have generally undergone this treatment. *Falanga* is almost always accompanied by other inflictions of pain on the prisoner. In general five or six men are engaged in the torture of one prisoner. Common methods accompanying *falanga* are: pouring water down the mouth and nose while the prisoner is screaming from pain; putting "Tide" soap in the eyes, mouth and nose; banging the head on a bench or on the floor; beating on other parts of the body, etc.

2. Numerous incidents of sexually-oriented torture were reported. In the case of women, the torturers shove as many fingers as possible, or an object, into the vagina and twist and tear brutally. This is also done with the anus. A tube is inserted into the anus and water is driven into the prisoner under very high pressure. In the case of men, beating on the genitals with long, thin sandbags have frequently been reported. One trade unionist was beaten so much that a testicle was driven up into his body.

3. Techniques of gagging are frequently reported. The throat is grasped in such a way that the windpipe is cut off, or a filthy rag (often soaked in urine) is shoved down the throat. Suffocation is prevented only at the last moment.

4. Beating on the head with sandbags or beating the head against the wall or floor are standard procedure. Many cases of concussion have been reported.

5. Beating naked flesh with wires knotted together into a whip.

6. Prisoners have been hung up for long periods of time. Usually the wrists are tied behind the back and the prisoner is suspended from the wrists.

7. Jumping on the stomach.

8. Tearing out the hair from the head and from the pubic region.

9. Rubbing pepper on sensitive areas of the body, such as the genitals, underarms, eyes, nose, etc.

10. Pulling-out toe-nails and finger-nails.

11. Different methods of inflicting burns, including putting-out cigarettes on parts of the body.

12. Use of electric shock. This is done at Military Hospital 401 and unconfirmed reports state that it is done at the Asphalia Station at Bouboulinas.

Physical beatings by the army and police as a method of intimidation and interrogation are general. Physical beating can be classified as torture if it is done in a systematic way. One man of over sixty contacted by the Delegation was beaten at regular intervals for more than 12 hours. He suffered broken ribs but reported that young people were beaten steadily for periods of up to five days. Generally from four to six men beat a prisoner with their fists and kick with their booted feet, or use instruments such as planks, pipes, canes, etc. At the Dionysos camp, which houses Greece's elite soldiers, prisoners are made to run a gauntlet. A reliable secondhand report from this camp is that a man literally had his eye knocked out of his head. The Amnesty International Delegation spoke with others who had broken ribs, noses, ear-drums, etc.

B. *Non-Physical Torture*

Many informants who have undergone torture consider that the non-physical methods were more difficult to bear.
1. Certain prisoners are intentionally moved to cells within ear-shot of other prisoners who are being violently interrogated. This has caused a number of nervous break-downs. One informant said that listening to the cries of the others was worse than undergoing the torture, one wanted to run in and be beaten rather than listen to the sufferings of another. It is reported that Mikis Theodorakis, the composer, who was never physically tortured, suffered a nervous collapse under this method.

2. Conditions of detention in some places are particularly bad. One technique is to leave the prisoner in a tiny, dark cell, without food, water or blankets, for some days. The cells at Dionysos, which are cut into the side of Mount Pendelli, have 10 centimetres of water in them all the time. There is an iron bench in the cell. As prisoners held here are not allowed to go out of the cells, the water is filled with their own excrement. The cells in the basement of Bouboulinas used for solitary confinement are full of vermin.

3. Threats to kill, maim and rape. People who had been tortured were often told that it would be repeated at a certain hour in the night, and were kept in constant terror by threats that they would have to undergo again what they had just experienced.

4. Stripping prisoners naked is particularly effective in Greece, where the association of nakedness with shame is very strong in the culture.

5. Mock executions were frequently reported. The prisoner faces a firing-squad, is blindfolded and the rifles are fired. Some prisoners experienced this more than once. It is often done at Kesaryni, in the place where war-time executions took place.

6. Signing Declarations is considered by many to be the most inhuman technique of the regime. Compulsion to sign a paper denouncing parents, wife or political beliefs particularly affects a person of highly developed conscience and ideals. This is used in a deliberate way to break down the spirit of the prisoner. The expert in these matters is Mr. Tournas, promoted to be Director of Greek Prisons under the regime. He begins by getting the prisoner to sign something innocuous, then tears up the paper, and makes the prisoner renounce more and more that he holds sacred. The Delegation interviewed people who had signed under this pressure, and all were in some sense broken. One particularly moving case was that of a man who signed in order to be free to see his daughter who

was dying of cancer. She died before he was released and he has had a nervous breakdown.

The Security Police and the Military Police are unrestricted today in Greece. Since, in Mr. Pattakos's words, "the laws sleep," the police may arrest anyone, in any place, at any time, with no obligation to charge him or inform anyone of his arrest. Believing that their own position is threatened by opposition to the Government, they have reacted brutally to those engaged in opposition. Those who have particularly suffered at the hands of the security forces are the young people, those who are not known abroad, and those believed to be of the left.

27 January, 1968

Amnesty International
Turnagain Lane
Farringdon Street
London, E. C. 4

This report received considerable attention in the European press. Its credibility was understandably limited by the fact that it was not possible to give the names of those tortured whom the delegates interviewed. Two months after this report, in one of those inexplicable decisions by the junta, Mr. Marreco was invited to return to Greece by the Deputy Prime Minister and Minister of the Interior, Stylianos Pattakos. It is believed that this was arranged through diplomatic channels and through the personal intervention of Mr. Francis Noel-Baker, M.B., a large landholder in Greece and one of the regime's stoutest defenders abroad.

Mr. Marreco arrived at the Athens airport only to be told by the chief officer there that he was "an unwelcome visitor" and would be put on the first plane leaving Athens. After the first Amnesty report his name was put on a black list. Mr. Marreco said that that simply would not do. He had been invited by General Pattakos, whom he insisted on calling immediately. The man said no calls were permitted and he disappeared. He came back and said that General Pattakos could not be reached, and relented to the extent of allowing Mr. Marreco to call his Embassy. The British Consul arrived with food and blankets. Finally after six hours, during which Pattakos argued with his reluctant colleague, Colonel Ladas, Mr. Marreco was allowed to enter Greece.

TORTURE OF POLITICAL PRISONERS IN GREECE

Second Report by Amnesty International

On 27 January Amnesty International, following an investigation carried out in Greece throughout the month of January, published a report on allegations that the Greek Government is practising the infliction of pain as an aid to interrogation. The Amnesty International Delegation had examined 16 witnesses who had been released and were at liberty in Athens and was satisfied that these people had been tortured. The witnesses were mostly members of Democratic Defence, the resistance organisation of the Centre Union Party. Many of them were students who had been arrested while distributing leaflets and had been tortured to reveal the names of their friends. These witnesses impressed the Delegation as being reliable and truthful. In addition, the Delegation obtained the names of 32 other prisoners still in prison whose families and professional advisors claimed that they had been tortured.

When the Report was circulated at Strasbourg, Amnesty International had in its hands the names and case histories of all the witnesses upon whom it relied in confirming the allegations which had been made. However, in the majority of cases, the Delegation had given its promise not to reveal the names of the witnesses because they were fearful of reprisals. Promises given had to be kept and it was decided that in all cases of people who had been released the risk of giving names was too great. In consequence, the Greek Government, through its official spokesmen, were able to attack the veracity of the Report on the grounds that no witnesses were named.

Nevertheless, as a result of certain influential representations which had been made to the Greek Government, that they should pay serious attention to the Amnesty International Report and take steps to satisfy world opinion as to the allegations of torture, Mr. Anthony Marreco, a member of the English Bar who had conducted the January investigation, was invited to return to Athens on 26 March to meet the Deputy Prime Minister and Minister of the Interior, Mr. Stylianos Pattakos. Mr. Marreco had meetings with Mr. Pattakos on 28, 29 March and 1 April and during his visit was given by Mr. Pattakos every facility to inspect any prison he wished and talk to any prisoner he wished to see.

On the evening of 28 March, Mr. Marreco visited the Police (Asphalia) Headquarters at Bouboulinas Street, Athens. He asked to see only one prisoner, Andreas Lendakis, 32, an archaeological student who was arrested in October 1967 as a member of the Patriotic Front (communist). This prisoner refused to answer the question whether or not he had been tortured and was unwilling to talk about his experiences beyond saying that he was ill. Mr. Marreco, however, had little doubt from his general demeanour that he had suffered extreme brutality. When a prisoner is asked if he has been tortured, he will surely answer "no" if this is not the case, if only because he is even more likely to suffer reprisals if he lies than if he tells the truth. When a prisoner refuses to answer, this seems to raise at least a justifiable presumption that he has been tortured. Before leaving the Bouboulinas Street Headquarters Mr. Marreco was allowed to accompany Lendakis back to his cell, which was one of a number of underground cells without any light at all or adequate ventilation, which may be tolerable for a prisoner held for a night or two but is quite unsuitable for the detention of prisoners for periods up to two or three months for which these cells have been used. Mr. Marreco also inspected the terrace and rooftop building which, it has been widely alleged, have been used as the place of torture. These buildings were exactly as described in the statements taken from the 16 witnesses who had been released, but beyond this fact no evidence was found either to prove or disprove the allegations.

On 30 and 31 March, Mr. Marreco visited respectively the prisons of Averoff and Aegina. At each prison he asked to see a number of prisoners who were brought to him in the presence of the Governor of the prison and an officer of the Police. He had not named in advance the prisoners he intended to see, so that the authorities had no warning which witnesses would be called. In both prisons the attitude of the witnesses was different from that of the man still in the hands of the Police. Out of a total of 12 prisoners seen, nine said quite definitely that they had been tortured and one said that he preferred not to answer the question. In each case the story they told corroborated all previous evidence as to place and the names of the torturers. The interrogation had taken the form of severe beating on the soles of the feet (Falanga) or Electric Shock treatment, the contacts being applied to the ears and other parts of the body.

Amongst the prisoners seen at Averoff Prison were Gerassimos Notaras, 31, an internationally respected economist and research fellow at the Social Science Centre of Athens, formerly assistant lecturer in the Political Science Faculty of the University of Lausanne; Constantine Sophoulis, 30, economist and grandson of a former Prime Minister, and Charalambos Protopapas, 45, Assistant Secretary-General of the Greek League for Human Rights. These men were Centre Union members of Democratic Defence who were arrested in October 1967. Sophoulis, who has not been tortured himself, confirmed the rumours which have been widely reported in the press that Notaras was removed from the prison on 8 February to the Royal Hellenic Navy vessel "Elli" lying near Scaramanga, where they were interrogated under torture in connection with an alleged Democratic Defence organisation which had been discovered in the Navy. Sophoulis said that when Notaras returned to the prison and for ten days after his return his physical and mental condition was clear evidence of the treatment he had suffered. He was unable to speak and barely able to walk. Notaras himself told Mr. Marreco that he had suffered electric shock treatment during 48 hours. Protopapas was unwilling to answer questions. The remainder of the prisoners seen both at Averoff and Aegina were known to be communists. Making all possible allowance for the possibility that some of these men were either describing tortures suffered at some earlier period in their lives and under previous governments and also for the possibility that the communists have been instructed to exaggerate the brutality of the treatment they have suffered (an explanation which Mr. Pattakos had suggested) Mr. Marreco found it impossible to avoid the conclusion that what the witnesses told him was substantially correct.

In talking to the prisoners, Mr. Marreco was also impressed by the measure of psychological terror which certain prisoners continually suffer by reason of their fear that at any moment the Security Police may return and take them away for further questioning. At least one of the witnesses described the terrible mental effect of being kept in a cell for days in solitary confinement within earshot of the place where other prisoners were being tortured.

On 1 April Mr. Marreco had his third meeting with the Deputy Prime Minister and Minister of the Interior at which he had to inform Mr. Pattakos that following his investigation he considered that there is at least prima facie evidence that the following prisoners have been tortured:

Dakos, Apostolos, tortured on or about 27/10/67 at Asphalia, Bouboulinas Street, Athens.

Karantinos, Panaiotis, tortured on or about 16/6/67 and 30/7/67 at Asphalia, Bouboulinas Street, Athens, by or in the presence of Mr. Karapanaiotis.

Karatsis, Charalambos, tortured on or about 1/11/67 at Asphalia, Aghiou Spiridonos, Aegaleo.

Lendakis, Andreas, tortured in October 1967 at Asphalia, Bouboulinas Street, Athens.

Notaras, Gerassimos, tortured in February/March 1968 on board the Royal Greek Naval Vessel "Elli".

Papaianakis, Christos, tortured on or about 19/10/67 at Asphalia, Piraeus, by or in the presence of Mr. Gianakopoulos, Mr. Sotiris Kouvas, Mr. Loukas Laroutsos, Mr. Panaiotis Angelopoulos, Mr. Kanatas, Mr. Fotinopoulos.

Protopapas, Charalambos, tortured in October/November 1967 at Asphalia, Bouboulinas Street, Athens.

Stratis, Giannis, tortured in September 1967 at Averoff Prison, by or in the presence of Major Theophiloianakis and Captain Kritikos, and on or about 1/10/67 at Dionysos Military Camp, by or in the presence of Sergeant Taxiarchis and 2 Military Police Corporals.

Syderis, Leonidas, tortured in September 1967 at Asphalia, Plateia Amerikis, Kypseli, by or in the presence of Mr. Lambrou, Mr. Panagopoulos, Mr. Mallios.

Xakoulakos, Giannis, tortured on or about 5/5/67 at Asphalia, Aghiou Spiridonos, Aegaleo, by or in the presence of Mr. Zagouras and Mr. Kapoiannis.

Mr. Marreco suggested that the Greek Government should immediately either order a Public Inquiry or institute criminal proceedings against certain officials named, if only to clear their reputation.

Mr. Pattakos's reply was a complete denial that the allegations are or can be true. He said that he has complete confidence in his officials and that the evidence given to Mr. Marreco is a tissue of lies from beginning to end, typical of communist propaganda. He said that all the witnesses including Notaras are known communists who have plotted violence against the Greek people. After prolonged and, at moments, heated argument, in which Mr. Marreco repeatedly told Mr. Pattakos that in all sincerity he was convinced that the allegations are substantially true and at least call for serious investigation, and that the political affiliations of the prisoners cannot in any sense be a justification of the treatment they claim to have suffered, Mr. Pattakos maintained that there are no grounds for further investigation. Mr. Marreco pointed out that unless the allegations are disproved Greece must inevitably face expulsion from the Council of Europe.

Pattakos: "Let them throw us out."

Anthony Marreco: "Is that what you wish me to go back to London and say?"

Pattakos: "You force me to say it. The Greek Government has to protect its people against its communist enemies. A communist is not a Greek. We must put our own security first."

II. THE INTERNATIONAL COMMITTEE OF THE RED CROSS

The International Committee of the Red Cross is a Swiss humanitarian organization concerned with the application of the Geneva Conventions. [There is frequent confusion between the "International Red Cross" and the "International Committee of the Red Cross," as they are often used interchangeably. The International Red Cross included the International Committee of the Red Cross, a Swiss neutralist institution founded in 1863; the League of Red Cross Societies, founded in 1919, which incorporates the Red Cross, Red Crescent and Red Lion and Sun Societies; and the National Red Cross (Red Crescent and Red Lion and Sun) Societies. The Committee tends to direct its relief effort to war and the League to natural disasters. Every four years there is a meeting of the International Conference of the Red Cross, the supreme deliberative body of the IRC.] The four conventions of August 12, 1949, provide for the protection of victims of war. [The four Conventions of August 12, 1949, are: "Amelioration of the Condition of the Wounded and Sick in Armed Forces in the Field," "Amelioration of the Condition of Wounded, Sick and Shipwrecked Members of the Armed Forces at Sea," "Treatment of Prisoners of War," and "Protection of Civilian Persons in Time of War."] The Committee not only intervenes during a "state of war" to assure that the Conventions are respected, but it serves as a relief agency for war victims. Its action in Biafra was an example. One hundred twenty-three states are parties to these Geneva Conventions. [Twenty-four states, including the U.S.A. and the U.S.S.R. have ratified the Conventions or acceded to them with reservations.]

In recent years the Committee has tentatively extended its humanitarian mission to certain situations in which there are political prisoners who do not fall within the scope of the Conventions because no "state of war" exists. In the last eleven years the Red Cross has offered its services or asked to visit political detainees in fifty-four countries suffering either *"troubles interieurs"* or *"tensions interieurs."* Forty-two of these states accepted. Five hundred ninety visits were made to some three hundred detention centers, and it is estimated that over one hundred thousand political prisoners have been visited. [This data was provided by the ICRC from a forthcoming book by Jacques Moreillon.]

The Committee was active in Greece during the Civil War and its aftermath, though it encountered many difficulties during the Civil War. A statement from an ICRC publication reviewing this period in Greece well expresses the philosophy of the ICRC: "To the Committee, all detainees, whether military or civilian, men and women indicted for various offenses or interned because of their political attitude, were persons at least entitled to humane treatment." [*Summary Report on the Work of the ICRC,* "Greece" ICRC, 1953, Geneva.] The Committee visited detention camps and prisons, engaged in relief work by sending and distributing tons of foodstuffs, clothing, and medical suppplies, and was active in repatriating Greeks. The ICRC continued to visit the dwindling number of political detainees until 1963, when there were no longer any prisoners detained under administrative order.

A few days after the military coup of April 21, a delegate of the International Committee of the Red Cross, through the Hellenic Red Cross Society, met with the Greek Prime Minister and the Minister of the Interior. The ICRC was given permission to visit places of detention. By the summer of 1969 the Committee had made six official missions to Greece, in which they visited political prisoners in island deportation camps, prisons, and hospitals.

The standard procedure of the ICRC is to submit to the government confidential reports, which include findings on prison conditions and recommendations for improvements where a minimum standard is not met. The Red Cross acts with absolute discretion, and its reports are made public only if the receiving government itself chooses to make them public. However, if the government publishes part of a report, especially in a misleading or tendentious fashion, the ICRC has the right to publish the entire document. The number of reports is secret, and one does not officially know, especially on the question of torture, what is in the reports that the Greek government has chosen not to make public.

The Greek government first used ICRC findings to refute torture charges after the appearance of the Amnesty report. They published reports that dealt with the conditions in island detention camps. There had never been any charges that torture took place in these camps, but rather that it occurred in police stations and army camps during interrogation. The Chief Delegate of the ICRC in Greece, Laurent Marti, had requested permission from the Greek authorities to visit places where torture was allegedly practiced. He was given permission to visit the Bouboulinas Street *Asphalia.* He went there on March 22, 1968. (This was six days before the visit of Mr. Marreco.) The following is the report he made of his visit. [Comite International de la Croix Rouge, *Rapport General sur les visites effectuees par les Delegues du Comite International de la Croix-Rouge Aux Detenus Politiques en Gerce. Mai 1967–Mars 1968,* pp. 17–20. Translation by the author.]

Political Detainees in the Hands of the Police Authorities

1. Since the first of the visits begun in May, 1967, in administrative deportation camps, the ICRC has received from various quarters information according to which a certain number of persons apprehended for political offenses have suffered * ill-treatment during police interrogation.

   According to this information, which has been corroborated by the declaration of the detainees (both accused and condemned) with whom the delegate of the ICRC, Mr. L. Marti, spoke, these ill-treatments have taken the following forms: †

   The most serious (*falanga*) is said to have consisted of beating the soles of the feet with a blunt object while the victim is lying on a bench, bound hand and foot; the most benign is said to have consisted of blows with the hand. Neither one nor the other has left marks. Ten detainees declared that they had undergone *falanga* several times, 12 others once, and 24 others said they only suffered blows with the hand. Eighty-five detainees have declared that they had been correctly treated.

---

*Translator's note: The verbs in the French original throughout the report are in the conditional tense.
†The ICRC delegate has spoken with 105 political detainees. At Aegina Prison, 50 out of 79 detainees were heard, the others having made it known that they had no complaints to make.

2. The detainees interrogated have declared that the large majority of the ill-treatment has been administered at the Central Police Station, located at Bouboulinas Street in Athens. The prisoners have particularly made the following declarations:

a) Any person arrested for a political or a common-law reason is placed in a basement of Bouboulinas Street for a period ranging from a few hours to several days. This transfer place, according to them, is completely insalubrious, deprived of light and air. The period spent in this basement "in company of criminals, drug addicts and prostitutes" has, according to their own declarations, strongly marked the prisoners.

b) The persons arrested for political offenses are then transferred to the Fourth Floor of the same building and lodged in cell-rooms for a period of 3 to 40 days.

c) Every night, according to some, several times a week according to others, screams have come from the terrace of the building, located above the fourth floor and where tortures were carried out, in particular the *falanga*. Hearing these screams constituted in itself a torture of a psychological nature.

d) At the bottom of the stairway leading to the terrace one is said to find a sign stating "Strictly forbidden to go up," which, according to the prisoners, indicates that the terrace is "out of bounds."

e) The tortures and especially *falanga* were carried out in an isolated place built on the terrace in which was found a "couch" or "bench." According to some prisoners, the place was not furnished, according to others it was cluttered with different objects and gave the impression of a junkroom.

f) Three prisoners have shown to the ICRC delegate some scars coming from—according to their declarations—the tortures they underwent.

3. Following his visits the ICRC delegate reported the above observations to the Minister of Justice, Mr. Kalambokias. The Minister has noted that the diet as well as the deteriorated condition of the places of incarceration have been the objects of complaints on the part of the prisoners.

Concerning the mistreatment suffered by persons interrogated before their incarceration, the Minister pointed out that only the Minister of Public Order was competent in this field. However he affirmed that he had participated at ministerial meetings during which very precise instructions were given to police chiefs forbidding them any use of torture and threatening to punish any guilty person.

4. For his part, Mr. Tzevelekos, Minister of Public Order, took account of the observations, particularly those which concern the tortures administered at Bouboulinas Street. He affirmed that very precise instructions had been given to police services forbidding mistreatment of any kind, no matter what.

The Minister declared that he did not know about the existence of a torture place on the terrace of the police station. The ICRC delegate asked him to be able to visit the Bouboulinas Street station and this was granted. He then asked him for the authorization to open the doors that he would designate, which was granted.

Mr. Tzevelekos insisted on making clear that the building was in a run-down condition and that he was planning to buy a modern building better adapted to their needs.

5. The ICRC delegate visited the police station at Bouboulinas Street on Friday afternoon, March 22. The director, Mr. Papaspiripoulos, asked one of his assistants to accompany the delegate and to open all the doors that the delegate would designate.

6. In the course of this visit, the following observations were made:

   a) The entire building is extremely run-down.

   b) The basement, which served as a transfer place, is totally unsuitable for a stay of even short duration. A real dungeon, it is covered with a nearly opaque skylight and lacks ventilation.

   Around the central courtyard are placed a dozen cells without window or furniture where some prisoners were confined, but which were open the day of the visit. According to the declarations that were made to the ICRC delegate, there were no political detainees in this basement.

   c) On the fourth floor was a certain number of cell-rooms where persons arrested for political offenses are said to have in fact lived for periods ranging from 2 to 40 days. Only one room was occupied the day of the visit, and that by two detainees.

   d) On the same floor, at the continuation of the central staircase, the delegate of the Red Cross recognized the few steps leading up to the terrace. The sign, "Strictly forbidden to go up," was in fact at the place described by the prisoners. When asked what had necessitated putting up this sign, the escort declared that it had been necessary to prevent a useless coming and going on this terrace "where there are various storerooms containing material that belongs to the bachelor employees of the police station."

   e) The terrace as well as the rest of the building corresponds to the description made by the detainees, who nevertheless did not point out that it is surrounded on three sides by apartment buildings (one of which is under construction) that rise above it by two to three floors.

   f) Five small juxtaposed rooms (*"locaux"*) are constructed on this terrace. They contain a large number of disparate objects, (scrap iron, furniture, bedsprings) but their closeness does not permit the installation of a bench or couch. Moreover, the wormeaten doors are generally in such bad condition that they close poorly, leaving spaces at the top and bottom.

   g) A shower room, very much larger, follows. The doors are not in any better condition. Its existence was not mentioned by any prisoner.

   h) The two persons arrested for political offenses who were in a fourth-floor room and whom the ICRC delegate questioned without any other witness except the interpreter of the Hellenic Red Cross, have affirmed that they have heard no cries coming from the terrace. The detainees said that they didn't know anything about torture being carried out there. To the question of whether or not they knew if tortures were inflicted in the basement of the building, they answered that they didn't know. They themselves had no complaint to make of this nature.

7. The delegate asked the director of the Police Station, Mr. Papaspiropoulos, if he could affirm that no mistreatment and no torture had been inflicted on prisoners at Bouboulinas Street.

   The Director answered that in certain cases the prisoners had received "slaps or blows" at the moment of or shortly after their arrest.

"However, I affirm that the prisoners who have stayed in Bouboulinas Street have not had to undergo any physical or psychological torture," he added.

The International Committee of the Red Cross limits itself to reporting these contradictory declarations from which it does not feel it has to draw conclusions about the reality of the alleged tortures.

It will continue its humanitarian action in favor of the political deportees and detainees in Greece, to the extent that authorizations to visit will still be given. Its delegates will remain attentive to the living conditions provided for the political detainees and particularly the treatment that is given them.

Excerpts from this report appeared in the government-controlled Greek press with the interpretation that the report "effectively demolishes the malicious allegations about torture." [Press release of the Ministry of the Prime Minister, May 23, 1968.] Though the report limited itself to presenting the two sides and the observations of the delegate during his visit, his observations were interpreted by most as indicating that in his judgment it was illogical and thus very unlikely that torture could have taken place on the *terratza*.

The growing public controversy over torture was something that the ICRC clearly preferred to avoid. It was a complex subject with important political implications, and involvement by the Committee could only place in jeopardy their major work in Greece, that of ameliorating the conditions of imprisonment. As the only foreign organization authorized to visit places of detention, the ICRC believed that its principal obligation was to the detainees. If recommendations of the ICRC were carried out by the government, this could only represent a benefit for the prisoners, a benefit that would not be gained in the absence of the ICRC. The Red Cross felt that their policy had already borne considerable fruit in Greece with the evacuation of the barren island of Yaros and the freeing of four hundred aged and sick prisoners.

The Red Cross has been criticized in general on the torture issue and in particular for having made the Bouboulinas report. The critics argue that the Red Cross should either have made a complete and thorough investigation of the torture charges or not dealt with the issue at all. By being allowed to visit only one alleged torture place and then only with advance notice, and not being allowed to visit others, such as the Dionysos Military Camp, nothing was really proved. This was a half-way measure which was worse than abstaining entirely, since the Bouboulinas report was used by the Greek government to deny the existence of tortures. Because the prestigious name of the Red Cross was associated with a denial of torture, an important segment of public opinion was misled.

The Committee, which bases its work on absolute discretion, has been placed in an awkward position by the Greek regime's persistence in using it to deny charges of mistreatment. The use by the regime of the first report of the ICRC in a pamphlet entitled "The Truth About Greece" [See section IV, "The Greek Government," p. 115.] was the object of a "vigorous protest" on the part of Mr. Marti when it came to his attention in July of 1968. A letter from the appropriate Greek authorities in September assured the ICRC that the pamphlet, as Mr. Marti had demanded, was withdrawn from circulation. The second incident which evoked a "vigorous protest" from the Red Cross was a declaration of the Foreign Minister, Mr. Pipinelis, on February 19, 1969:

> Athens News, February 20, 1969
> NO EVIDENCE OF TORTURE TURNED UP BY RED CROSS
> . . . "But what is of special importance to us," Pipinelis continued, "is the absolute silence of the I.R.C. envoy with regard to the so-called tortures allegedly inflicted on the detainees.
> "The Red Cross envoy has not only found nothing to substantiate these charges but on the contrary has stated that all the detainees he had seen, in the absence of any third party, had assured him that they had not been subjected to any maltreatment."

Mr. Marti, in Geneva at the time, flew to Greece in order to lodge his protest with the Foreign Minister. The statement that all the detainees had assured Mr. Marti they were not mistreated was simply a false statement. Mr. Pipinelis said that he had been misquoted (in the government-controlled press) and he promised to make public the report to which he was referring, a report which did not mention torture, as it never treated the problem.

On June 20, 1969, the dynamic Acting President of the ICRC, Prof. Jacques Freymond, had a meeting with Prime Minister Papadopoulos. As a result of the Greek experience and other similar ones, the ICRC believes that it must be made publicly clear that the ICRC is reporting only on those places where it is authorized to visit and actually visits. In a case like Greece, where it was refused access to some places of detention, the policy would be to demand of the government authorization to visit any police station without previous notice. If this was refused, then the ICRC would make it known that its secret reports were not making any judgment on mistreatment of prisoners in the hands of the police. If the government accepted, all well and good, the ICRC could extend its humanitarian work. Prof. Freymond is reported to have asked the Prime Minister for the right to visit without previous notice all police stations and military camps where detainees were being held.

This move by the ICRC coincided with the negotiations for a

"friendly settlement" before the European Commission of Human Rights. The Greek proposition was to present a "timetable" for a return to the rule of law and democratic government. However, it was clear that torture was not subject to any timetable acceptable to the Scandinavians and it would have to be stopped immediately. The Greek government proposed that it submit itself to international control, through the ICRC. It was in September that the negotiations with the ICRC gained momentum when the Greek government managed to obtain a draft of the Commission's report on torture. The Committee of Ministers of the Council of Europe was to discuss Greece's suspension on December 12, 1969, and Greek diplomacy needed something to offset this very condemning report. On November 3, 1969, the ICRC and the Greek government officially signed the following agreement:

"Agreement Between the Government of the Kingdom of Greece and the International Committee of the Red Cross

The Government of the Kingdom of Greece and the International Committee of the Red Cross, desiring to serve the principles of humanity and justice, have agreed as follows:

Visits to administrative deportees

The delegates of the International Committee of the Red Cross accompanied by their interpreters shall have access to all places occupied either permanently or temporarily by administrative deportees, i.e.: deportation camps, transfer centres, hospitals and infirmaries.

The conditions governing such visits shall be those hitherto in force and specified in the preceding reports.

Visits to accused and convicted persons in the hands of the judicial authorities

The delegates of the International Committee of the Red Cross accompanied by their interpreters shall have access to all prisons and all other places in the country where persons accused or convicted of political offences are detained.

The conditions governing such visits shall be those hitherto in force and specified in the preceding reports.

Visits to police stations

The delegates of the International Committee of the Red Cross accompanied by their interpreters shall have access to all police stations in the country where any persons are provisionally detained for preliminary enquiry into political offences so that they may form a personal opinion on the state of the premises and the conditions of detention.

Request for information

The delegates of the International Committee of the Red Cross shall be entitled, on the application of the families concerned, to apply to the police authority for information about arrested or detained persons in cases where their families have not been able to obtain such information directly from the competent authorities.

Such information shall relate more particularly to:
— the place of detention;
— the general nature of the offence;
— the conditions of detention;
— the possibility of visits by members of family or delegates of the International Committee of the Red Cross.

Reception of families

The International Committee of the Red Cross shall be entitled as in the past to receive persons related to detained persons for discussions of a family nature.

Material assistance to the families of detained persons

The International Committee of the Red Cross shall be entitled to arrange for one or more schemes of material assistance to necessitous families of persons who for any reason have been detained for more than two years.

All such schemes shall be undertaken in association and collaboration with the Ministry of Social Affairs and the Greek Red Cross.

Such assistance shall consist of articles of clothing, food, and pharmaceutical products, the greater part of which shall be purchased locally. The International Committee of the Red Cross may also provide through the competent authorities travelling tickets to necessitous families who have not so far been able to visit their relations in detention.

Organisation of the delegation of the International Committee of the Red Cross

The delegation of the International Committee of the Red Cross shall be permitted to occupy the necessary offices for its Secretariat and for the reception of families.

The appointment of delegates of the International Committee of the Red Cross and of the staff of its office shall be subject to the prior approval of the competent authorities.

The Government of the Kingdom of Greece shall appoint a senior official as a liason officer with the International Committee of the Red Cross. The International Committee of the Red Cross shall apply to this officer for the settlement of current problems arising in the course of the execution of their mission and for the purpose of obtaining such interviews as they may desire.

Declarations and publications

No declarations or publications on the above-mentioned points or the mission of the International Committee of the Red Cross in general shall be made without prior consultation between the Government of the Kingdom of Greece and the International Committee of the Red Cross. The International Committee of the Red Cross shall issue from its headquarters in Geneva periodic press communiqués stating the names of the places visited, the dates and the conditions of the visit (conversations in the absence of witnesses, etc.), the names of the delegates and a statement that the Report of the visit will be sent as is customary to the detaining authorities.

These communiqués shall not contain any expression of opinion on the position of the detained persons or the treatment they are receiving.

The other activities of the International Committee of the Red Cross in the country shall also be mentioned in the periodic communiqué.

Reports of visits

As customary, reports of visits shall be sent only to the detaining authorities. The Government of the Kingdom of Greece shall abstain from any partial publication of the report or any public statement of extracts from the reports.

As in the past and as is customary, the International Committee of the Red Cross shall express no opinion on the motives for internment or detention.

Entry into force and duration

This agreement shall enter into force on the third of November 1969. The agreement shall be valid for one year from the date of its entry into force and shall automatically be extended from year to year unless denounced by one of the contracting parties.

This is the first time that an agreement like this has been signed by a sovereign state in time of peace. Rather than reflecting a desire on the part of the Greek government to protect human rights or an admission that they are incapable themselves of protecting them, it reflects the great pressure from abroad over the question of torture. It still remains to be seen whether this agreement will be carried out and whether or not the two parties interpret it in the same way. The ICRC interprets it to mean that it gives them the right to see any prisoner and visit any place of detention without previous notice.

Between November 24 and December 3 the ICRC made an impressive number of visits to places of detention both under military and civilian control. [*CICR,* Geneve, Communique de presse No. 1039, 5 decembre 1969.] They were free to speak freely with any prisoner they designated. It appears that they presented in advance a program to the Greek government of their proposed visits. Consequently it would appear that the element of the agreement pertaining to no advance notice remains to be tested. Reports on these visits are to be given to the Greek authorities.

III. THE EUROPEAN COMMISSION
OF HUMAN RIGHTS

The "Greek Case" has been the most important case in the history of the European Human Rights Commission. [Up until 1967, the Commission had received 3001 individual applications and only three applications by states. One of the state applications was that of the

Greek government on behalf of Cypriots during the "emergency" of the late fifties. The Greek government claimed the Cypriots were deprived of human rights, among those the right not to be tortured. (Many of the arguments used by the Greek government during this time were used by the Scandinavians in the proceedings before the Commission, and the current Greek government had to argue against them.) The Report of the Commission was never made public as the two parties, Great Britain and Greece, reached a political settlement over the Cyprus question. After the Report on the Greek Case was made known in the British press at the end of November, 1969, the Greek government accused the British government of "leaking it," and said the British were in no position to talk about torture, when the archives of the Commission were full of their misdeeds in Cyprus. Those who have read the Report say that the only mistreatment found by the Commission was whipping, though now after ten years it is generally known that British methods went way beyond this.] Called upon to investigate whether or not Greece had violated almost all of the basic human rights guaranteed by the European Convention of Human Rights, the Commission concluded that the Greek regime was not fulfilling its obligations under the Convention and had in fact violated the many articles cited in the application of the Scandinavian governments. [The Commission went even further than the Scandinavian application in that they felt compelled to point out that at least five people may well have died as a result of mistreatment and therefore Article Two, not cited by the applicant states, was also violated. ("Everyone's right to life shall be protected by law. No one shall be deprived of his life intentionally save in the execution of a sentence of a court following his conviction of a crime for which this penalty is provided by law." Article Two [1])]

On November 4, 1969, the full Commission adopted its Report on the Greek Case. More than half of the twelve hundred pages of the Report deal with Article Three. ("No one shall be subjected to torture or to inhuman or degrading treatment or punishment.") It was on this Article that the Commission was most able to act like a court. Over a two year period, the jurists heard fifty-eight witnesses, including tortured and torturers, they visited some places where torture was alleged to have been carried out, they heard oral argument from the lawyers of both sides on every issue, and received hundreds of documents. The Report gives the names of 213 people who were mistreated and names five persons who died as a result of mistreatment. The fifteen jurists of the Commission held unanimously that Article 3 had been violated.

The Report is a historic step in international human rights law, as it is perhaps the first time that an international body carried out such a thorough investigation of a police state. The horror of the situation emerges vividly from the Report, despite its legal and technical style. Another aspect that emerges is the extraordinary ineptitude of the Greek authorities in handling this case. Especially when the sub-Commission heard evidence in Greece, the confusion of the authorities is manifest. They let the jurists see some witnesses and places and then refused them others. Documents such as police ledgers and medical reports were patently falsified. The Greek government witnesses and lawyers seemed to believe that the argument, "It is a communist lie" was a sufficient and effective rebuttal to the mass of evidence produced by the Scandinavians. It is clear that the Greek authorities, unaccustomed to the rule of law in their own country, were totally unprepared for the rigors of a proper hearing.

The following include a summary of the major findings of the Report, the "Opinion of the Commission," which is at the end of the volume of the Report dealing with torture, and some extracts and anecdotes from the Report.

Major Findings

1. "The Commission has found it established beyond doubt that torture or ill-treatment contrary to Article 3 has been inflicted in a number of cases." Given the "repetition of acts" and the "official tolerance" of these acts, the practice of torture constitutes an "administrative practice."

2. There was not on April 21, 1967, a communist danger of an overthrow of constitutional government, nor was there a breakdown in public order which would constitute "public emergency threatening the life of the nation."

3. "The Greek people are prevented from expressing their political opinions by choosing a legislature in accordance with Article 3 of the Protocol" (which guarantees "free elections at regular intervals").

4. The Greek regime has violated most of the fundamental freedoms guaranteed under the European Convention of Human Rights pertaining to freedom of expression, association, fair trial, effective remedy, etc.

Opinion of the Commission[1]

A. General

1. The Commission, in evaluating the evidence obtained by the Sub-
Commission and set out in the preceding parts, treats the statements
of alleged victims of torture or ill-treatment, who have testified on
oath or solemn declaration and in person, as the more direct evidence.

In a number of further cases the Sub-Commission had decided to sum-
mon the alleged witnesses and these were prevented by the respondent
Government from giving oral evidence but written statements were
received which were corroborated by other evidence (Part II above).
Similar corroboration was also obtained in a number of further cases,
where the alleged victims had not yet been summoned when the Sub-
Commission decided to terminate its investigation.

Finally there is the group of all further cases of alleged torture or
ill-treatment raised throughout the proceedings but where no substantial evidence was received, and these are set out in Annex V to
this volume of the report.

2. The Commission has examined a mass of documentary evidence presented to it. This documentary evidence varies much in authority,
credibility and relevance and includes official reports and medical
certificates and records, presented by the respondent and applicant
Governments; reports of the International Committee of the Red Cross
on visits of its delegates to various establishments where political detainees were held; reports and statements by persons acting on behalf
of the Consultative Assembly, by members of foreign parliaments and
by journalists, and reports by private investigators, some of whom also
testified before the Sub-Commission.

3. The Commission has also taken into account much testimony, including that of police officers and other authorities, denying the infliction of torture or ill-treatment in particular cases or in general.
Such testimony has also been presented by or on behalf of certain
alleged victims.

Here it must be remarked that the respondent Government has in
certain cases not responded in any form to the allegations made in
the present proceedings: that is to say, it has not proposed witnesses
or presented documents or indicated other evidence, to counter the
allegations [2] or has simply ignored them. In other cases it has limited
itself to a brief, general denial,[3] and has invoked in support the state-

---

[1]Mr. Eustathiades did not participate in the deliberations and votes on Chapter IV
concerning Article 3 of the Convention.
[2]In particular in the cases of those heard as witnesses in June and July 1969: Vardikos, Vlassis, Korovessis, Pangopoulou, Tsirka.
[3]cf. respondent Government's memorial of 15th November, 1968, listing 54 cases
without generally even indicating the date and place of arrest of the person concerned.

ments of certain members of foreign parliaments and other public figures. These statements have little weight with the Commission for two reasons: first, they are largely generalities or statements of opinion; secondly, where they are directed to particular cases there is no indication that they were based on methods of inquiry or standards of proof that the Commission considers necessary in such cases.

4. Account has also been taken of the fact that the persons detained for political activities or offences since April 1967 have in the great majority of cases been avowed Communists or members of the EDA party or persons collaborating with them. For this reason the Commission has kept in mind the possibility that accounts of torture or ill-treatment might be fabricated as part of Communist or anti-government propaganda, or to justify, in the eyes of their associates, confessions or disclosures of information made by detainees.

5. In this connection the Commission finds two features common to many of the accounts of torture or ill-treatment: the use of *falanga,* and, in particular, its use in the washroom and the 'terrazza' in Bouboulinas Street. Not all accounts of the washroom and the 'terrazza' mention the same features, and there are sometimes errors. Thus some describe the small wall outside the washroom; the boiler, the sink with the metal lid, and the back door in the washroom; and the notice on the stairs leading to the 'terrazza': others do not mention them or say they did not notice them. In two cases, the number of rooms and doors in the building on the 'terrazza' is wrongly described.[4]

6. *Falanga* or bastinado has been a method of torture known for centuries. It is the beating of the feet with a wooden or metal stick or bar which, if skilfully done, breaks no bones, makes no skin lesions, and leaves no permanent and recognisable marks, but causes intense pain and swelling of the feet. The use of *falanga* has been described in a variety of situations: on a bench or chair or on a car-seat; with or without shoes on. Sometimes water has been thrown over the feet and sometimes the victim has been made to run around between beatings. Victims have also been gagged.

7. The Commission considers that the variety of situations in which *falanga* is described as being used, and the differences and errors of description of the washroom and 'terrazza,' far from putting in question the veracity and reality of the accounts, tend to confirm them. For it is natural that, where several witnesses describe the same place or incident, there will be variations and errors of detail: indeed it is the precise repetition of the same features which would be suspect and would point to fabrication.

8. While *falanga* and severe beatings of all parts of the body are the commonest forms of torture or ill-treatment that appear in the evidence before the Sub-Commission, other forms have been described: for example, the application of electric shock, squeezing of the head in a vice, pulling out of hair from the head or pubic region, or kicking of the male genital organs, dripping water on the head, and intense noises to prevent sleep.

Falanga has not only been the commonest form of torture or ill-treatment in the case in which the Sub-Commission has been able to establish the facts to a substantial degree but also appears with great

---

[4]Tsirka and Korovessis: it should be noted that both were allegedly taken up at night-time. Vlassis, who gave evidence on the same day as Korovessis, but had been taken up in day-time, gave an accurate description.

frequency in the further allegations raised in the proceedings with
regard to other named detainees. The principal forms of alleged treatment—frequently several forms combined in one and the same case—
are as follows in the two categories:

	cases examined	further allegations
Falanga	23	53
Electro-shock	4	3
Mock execution or threats	12	15
to shoot or kill the victim		
Other beating or	26	172 [5]
ill-treatment		

9. While it is an important feature of *falanga* that it generally leaves no
   enduring marks, beating of the feet may break bones, damage or destroy the nails, or cause skin lesions. The Sub-Commission was denied
   the opportunity of investigating cases where the breaking of bones,[6]
   and the destruction of nails [7] were said to have taken place. There are
   witnesses who have testified to the Sub-Commission about the condition of the right ankle of Apostolos Dakos.[8]

B. Evidence of a practice of torture and ill-treatment

10. The Commission has found it established beyond doubt that torture
    or ill-treatment contrary to Article 3 has been inflicted in a number of
    cases.

    It will now apply to these cases. in the light of all the other evidence
    at its disposal, the criteria which it has chosen for determining whether
    they are part of a practice of torture or ill-treatment of political de-
    tainees in Greece since 21st April, 1967: namely, the repetition of acts
    and official tolerance of them.

11. It appears from the testimony of a number of witnesses [9] that a cer-
    tain roughness of treatment of detainees by both police and military
    authorities is tolerated by most detainees and even taken for granted.
    Such roughness may take the form of slaps or blows of the hand on
    the head or face. This underlines the fact that the point up to which

---

[5]This number includes 69 alleged cases—mostly mentioned in the list submitted by
the witness Papagiannakis. Verbatim Record (Athens) IV, p. 1076—where torture
has been alleged without further specification, it may therefore well include alleged
cases of falanga.

[6]e.g. Margaritis. Reklitis: in these cases the medical records were refused.

[7]e.g. Maria Kallerghi. Petropoulos, Kiaos; these persons were prevented from ap-
pearing before the Sub-Commission.

[8]cf. Part IV, case No. 3.

[9]Tambakis reported that both he and Athanassios Tsimboukis had received slaps
in the face but expressed their gratitude for the treatment to the police, Verbatim
Record (December 1968) I, p. 85, 91.

   cf. also the description of the respondent Government's permanent representative,
Mr. Vitsaxis. that this involved no discrepancy. ibid. p. 94. The Director of the Athens
Asphalia declared to the delegates of the International Red Cross in a general manner
that in certain cases the prisoners had received "slaps and blows" during, or shortly
after their arrest. cf. Red Cross Report. May 1967-March 1968. p. 20. cf. however, also
the evidence by Zervoulakos on the case of Dr. Vassilios Tsironis who when struck in
the face by a guard in Aegina Prison defended himself and lodged a denuniciation,
Verbatim Record (December 1968) I, p. 235.

prisoners and the public may accept physical violence as being neither cruel nor excessive, varies between different societies and even between different sections of them. However, the allegations raised in the proceedings generally concern much more serious forms of treatment which, if established, clearly constitute torture or ill-treatment.

12. The factor of *repetition of acts* of torture or ill-treatment appears in the concentration of incidents around the Asphalia (Security Police).

13. While complaints have been made as to the conditions of detention centres on the islands, virtually no allegations have been made of torture being inflicted in these places. Further, it is to be noted that, in complaints of torture or ill-treatment by the Asphalia, some witnesses have made a distinction between the uniformed guards and more senior officers, usually in plain clothes, and have spoken of help and kindness from the former.

14. Further, the Commission cannot ignore the sheer number of complaints. The International Red Cross reported that, at one stage, out of 131 prisoners, 46 complained of torture or ill-treatment,[10] and it apparently later investigated certain further torture allegations but the respondent Government has failed to submit the report on those investigations.[11] In the present proceedings allegations have been made concerning the treatment of 213 named detainees; 30 of these cases had been examined to some substantial degree before the proceedings were terminated following the respondent Government's refusal to make possible the hearing of a number of further witnesses detained in Greece.

Since the Commission considers that in 11 of the cases which were examined torture or ill-treatment has been established and that in 17 others there is at least some evidence corroborating the complaint, it is not able to reject the whole as a conspiracy by Communist and anti-Government groups to discredit the Government and the police. It cannot but regard the actual number of complaints brought before it as strong indication that acts of torture or ill-treatment are not isolated or exceptional, nor limited to one place.

15. As regards the factor of *official tolerance,* the Sub-Commission has taken into consideration the following factors:

(a) The general failure of the respondent Government to order enquiries, either administrative or judicial, into numerous allegations of torture or ill-treatment, where both victim and offender have been named and other circumstantial evidence provided, is remarkable. No Government could, in the view of the Commission, allow such allegations to stand unchallenged by proper enquiry without the inference being drawn that it is generally indifferent to them and therefore tolerates any torture or ill-treatment that does in fact take place.

Further, in sixteen individual cases in which administrative enquiries have been ordered, no enquiry has yet been carried out according to information provided by the respondent Government. In eight cases,[12] reports of enquiries made have been submitted and have already been examined under Article 13 of the Convention.[13] Such administrative

10General Report May 1967-March 1968, page 17.
11cf. Sub-Commission's requests of 7th and 19th February, 21st March, 25th April and 21st May, 1969.
12cf. Annex II to this volume of the Report.
13Volume I, p. 151, para. 305 (2) of this Report.

enquiries as have been ordered have thus either not been carried out, or have been inadequate in their conduct.

If, as the respondent Government as well as the officers conducting the enquiries and the police officers themselves claim, allegations of torture and ill-treatment are invented for the purpose of defaming the police, it is surprising that so little is done by the respondent Government to clear their name.

(b) The refusal of the respondent Government to allow a number of witnesses to appear before the Sub-Commission, whom it had selected precisely because there was in their cases concrete evidence capable of proof or disproof; and to produce to the Sub-Commission the report of the International Red Cross of August 1968 based upon its investigation of certain allegations of torture or ill-treatment.

16. The Sub-Commission has also received testimony from one witness, Lt. Commander Marotis [14] to the effect that torture and ill-treatment of detainees has even been authorised in a "circular" directive to security officers in the armed services.

The main purpose of the "circular" directive, as described, was to ensure that, in the inflicting of torture or ill-treatment, no physical marks should, as far as possible, be made, and it was said to have been signed by General Anghelis when Chief of Staff who, however, denied categorically ever having issued any special instruction as to how investigations should be carried out.[15] The Sub-Commission finds it inherently improbable that such a "circular" directive, purporting to authorise offences against the criminal law, would be issued over the name of a chief of staff or that, even if issued, it would be permitted to come into the hands of ordinary sailors such as Marotis' assistant.[16] It therefore rejects the existence of such a document.

C. Summary

17. The Sub-Commission has investigated 30 cases to a substantial degree and expressed some conclusion with regard to 28 of them.[17] With regard to these cases the Commission [18] finds it established that:

(i) torture or ill-treatment has been inflicted in 11 individual cases, namely: [19]

— Vardikos, Vlassis, Leloudas, Miss Arseni, Mrs. Tsirka, Lendakis, Korovessis (by the Athens Security Police)

— Veryvakis (at the headquarters of the Athens Suburban Gendarmerie in Patissia)

— Meletis, Miss Pangopoulou (by the Security Police of Salonica)

[14]Verbatim Record (November 1968) I, p. 55-57.
[15]Anghelis, Verbatim Record (Athens) 1. p. 312.
[16]cf. Marotis, Verbatim Record (November 1968) I, pp. 74 and 80.
[17]It refrained from expressing conclusions in the cases of Marketakis and Gavalas.
[18]Mr. Eustathiades did not participate in the deliberations and votes on Chapter IV concerning Article 3 of the Convention.
[19]Sub-sections (i) and (ii) were adopted by a majority of 12 members.

— Livanos (at the 521 Marines Brigade camp near Aghia Paraskevi)

(ii) there has since April 1967 been a practice of torture and ill-treatment by the Athens Security Police, Bouboulinas Street, of persons arrested for political reasons, and that: [19]

(a) this torture and ill-treatment has most often constituted in the application of *"falanga"* or severe beatings of all parts of the body;

(b) its purpose has been the extraction of information including confessions concerning the political activities and associations of the victims and other persons considered to be subversive;

(iii) the evidence before the Commission of torture or ill-treatment having been inflicted on 17 other individuals demands further investigation, since it ranges

from indications:

— Ambatielos (by the Piraeus Security Police)

— Karaosman (at the Interrogation Centre of the Central Intelligence Service in Aghia Paraskevi)

and the establishment of prima facie case:

— Miss Kallerghi, Petropoulos, Kiaos, Tsiloglou, Dakos (by the Athens Security Police)

— Notaras (by the Athens Security Police and on board the ship "Elli')

to strong indications:

— Xintavelonis, Mrs. Papanicola (at the Athens Security Police)

— Panagoulis (at the 505 Marine Brigade camp near Dionysos)

— Papagiannakis and Yotopoulos (by the Piraeus Security Police)

— Nestor, Sipitanos and Pyrzas (in a military camp near the Sedes airfield in Salonica—Central Intelligence Service).

The Sub-Commission was in effect prevented, directly or indirectly, by the respondent Government from completing its investigation of these cases;

(iv) the competent Greek authorities, confronted with numerous and substantial complaints and allegations of torture and ill-treatment, having failed to take any effective steps to investigate them or to ensure remedies for any such complaints or allegations found to be true.[20]

18. The Commission also finds that:

(i) the conditions of detention in the cells in the basement of the Security Police building in Bouboulinas Street, in which persons arrested for political reasons have been held, are contrary to Article 3; [21]

(ii) the combination of conditions described in Part VI above, in which political offenders are held in the Averoff Prison, and the extreme manner of the separation of detainees from their families and the conditions of gross overcrowding in the camps on Leros, also constitute breaches of Article 3.[22]

---

[20]Sub-sections (iii)—except the findings on 4 cases—and (iv) were adopted by a majority of 13 members. The findings on the cases of Ambatielos, Karaosman, Papagiannakis and Yotopoulos were adopted by a majority of 10 members.

[21]Sub-section (i) was adopted by a majority of 13 members.

[22]Sub-section (ii) was adopted by a majority of 11 members.

IV. THE GREEK GOVERNMENT

This pamphlet was published by the Press and Information Department of the Ministry to the Prime Minister in the spring of 1968. It was widely distributed until the ICRC requested that it be withdrawn from circulation.

The Truth
Regarding the Deported Communists
and the Alleged Tortures

INTERNATIONAL COMMUNISM launched on the morrow of the Revolution of April 24, 1967 an unprecedented vile attack about alleged torturing of political prisoners and their inhuman living conditions. These communist charges were comprised in a report of "Amnesty International" whose two representatives, Messrs. Anthony Mareko and James Becket, visited Greece from December 30, 1967, to January 26, 1968, following permission of the Greek government.

Messrs. Mareko and Becket came into contact, freely only with detained communists or their families. Their report contained two kinds of charges: a) Torturing of prisoners and, b) their inhuman living conditions. Having adopted the communist views without any investigation of the charges, "Amnesty International" drafted a report stressing the following inter alia:

> "Use of tortures has been made deliberately and officially. The places where the most serious ones were reported were General Security on Bouboulinas street, Military Hospital 401 and the Camp at Dionyssos. The usual initial torture is the so-called *"falanga."* The prisoner is tied to a bench and the soles of his feet are beaten with a stick or pipe. Numerous incidents of sexually-oriented torture were reported. Very often cases of gagging were reported, as well as beating on the head with sandbags and beating the naked flesh with a whip.

> Pulling-out nails and use of electric shock.

> The prisoners were hung for long periods. Rubbing sensitive parts of the body, with pepper. Jumping on the stomach".

In the face of these unprecedented and unfounded slanders of international communism and the fellow-travellers as well as of "Amnesty International", the Greek government has accepted that successive missions of distinguished International Red Cross representatives visit Greece and ascertain whether the charges were founded or not. In fact, from May 1967 to March 1968 four visits of representatives of the International Committee of Red Cross were made. These representatives proceeded to a long and free investigation of the alleged torturing and living conditions of political prisoners at Yaros, Leros, the prisons, as well as the different hospitals where they were treated.

In parallel, on April 15, a British five-member inter-party committee composed of Messrs. Gordon Bagier (Labour Party), Russell Johnston (Liberal Party), Anthony Beck and David Webster (Conservative Party) and Ted Garret (Labour Party) visited Greece in order to ascertain the living conditions of political prisoners. On the other hand another objective investigator, Mr. Francis Noël Baker, Labour M.P., has not hesitated to stigmatise in the British Parliament the lying and slandering campaign against the Greek government as regards the question of political prisoners.

Smashing Reply

The reply to the vile falsehoods of "Amnesty International" which is influenced by communism, has been really smashing. The slander was of two kinds: a) Tortures of satanic inspiration at the General Security in Bouboulinas street, at Military Hospital 401 and at Dionyssos, and b) inhuman living conditions of persons under administrative deportation.

1. *Torturing*

On the first score of the slanders, that is to say on torturing, there are three authoritative and serious investigators who reject the charges after a careful and completely free investigation. These are: a) The Committees of the International Red Cross

b) the report of the inter-party British Parliamentary Committee and

c) the distinguished British politician of international prestige, the Labour M.P., Mr. Francis Noël Baker.

The reports of the International Red Cross.

The reports of the International Committee of Red Cross, in substance, rejected the charges about torturing prisoners. They refused to take a stand, but they also denied the testimonies about alleged torturing in the building of the General Security. The International Red Cross Committee composed of distinguished personalities, in order to reach their conclusions, reported only narratives of political prisoners, all communists, in the prison of Aegina. Those displaced in the islands made no charges about tortures. The prisoners claimed that the greatest part of the alleged tortures were inflicted on them on the terrace of the central police building in Bouboulinas street. This view is rejected by the International Red Cross in its report which says verbatim: "The roof and the entire building correspond with the description of the prisoners who, however, do not mention that it is surrounded on three sides by in-

habited buildings which are higher by two or three storeys". All the
prisoners, however, according to the International Red Cross report, have
assured that they have heard no cry coming from the roof and that they
ignored that torturing was being inflicted. Also the fact that the slander
about tortures and the myths about inquisition with the hair-raising descriptions of the famous "Amnesty Committee" are confined in some
charges, made by some prisoners, to the torture of the *"falanga"*, even
which is not proved, constitutes the most eloquent proof of truth.

The findings of the inter-party Committee of British MPs.

The report of British MPs on the subject of tortures is equally smashing for the slanderers of Greece. On April 22, 1968, the five British MPs
Messrs. Antony Beck and David Webster (Conservative Party), Ted Garret and Gordon Bagier (Labour Party) and Russell Johnston (Liberal
Party) made an announcement to the Greek and foreign journalists at
the Grande Bretagne Hotel, stressing: "The claims of the foreign press
that tortures were inflicted on political prisoners at the police headquarters
are ridiculous. No political detainees could be tortured in the police
headquarters in Athens in full view of the people. Maybe there have been
isolated cases but even here it is difficult to distinguish between facts and
propaganda. At all events, we believe that no instructions from above
have been given about brutality and torturing and we have assurances
that any case of excessive zeal on the part of subaltern police members
shall be punished severely". Similarly, two of the British MPs in question
(Gordon Bagier and R. Jonhston) in another interview with Greek and
foreign journalists on April 26, 1968, stressed:

> "No claim whatever about ill-treatment of prisoners on Leros
> has been made. Glezos is in excellent health and did not com-
> plain of brutality. It is true that one of the deportees, Mr.
> Abatiellos, had a scar on his foot but, we are not in a position
> to say categorically whether it was caused by ill-treatment. In
> no circle did we find anyone, even in the camp, who was ready
> to accuse the rulers of Greece of conducting any brutality or
> cruelty to deportees. Citizens accept the government positively
> and say that it is a good government. Part of the foreign press
> is not objective. We believe that presentation of things by the
> Western press has been biased in one direction".

Mr. Francis Noël Baker.

Finally, the slanderers of Greece have received a heavy blow from
the Labour M.P., Mr. Francis Noël Baker, as regards the alleged tortures.

In the course of a debate on Greece in the House of Commons on
April 11, 1968, Mr. Francis Noël Baker gave the assurance that a friend
of his, a former EDA deputy, had confided to him that the treatment he
had while he was detained was exemplary. He said that the laws on
the strength of which individuals are detained in Greece, had been
voted by previous governments. Those who applied the law were the
same persons as before. Everybody hates tortures. But it is indispensable
to check facts so that there should be no doubt. The last report of
"Amnesty International" does not fulfil these prerequisites. It appears
that Mr. Mareko has strong political views and so restricted contacts in
Greece that it is impossible for him to make an objective appreciation
of things. He does not speak Greek and does not know the country.
Finally, Mr. Baker in a statement to the press on April 6, 1968, stressed
that reports about torturing of political prisoners in Greece had been
inflated to a superlative degree. Also, in another statement, when he
returned from Greece, Mr. Baker said characteristically: "In view of the

conclusions reached by a really responsible organisation, like the International Red Cross, I consider that the charges about brutal actions on the part of Greek police officers are being magnified in advance".

* * * *

Conclusion

— There has been slander on two scores: A) Inquisition-like tortures of political prisoners and B) Inhuman living conditions of deportees on Yaros-Leros.

— The charges had two sources: 1) Communist and fellow-travelling whispering propaganda and 2) The report of "Amnesty International" attempting to confirm communist slander.

— On the other hand, there have been a) responsible statements by representatives of the Greek government at various times denying the slanders with concrete data. b) The reports of the International Red Cross. c) the statements of the British inter-party Committee of MPs who visited the places of detention of deportees, and d) the statement of the British Labour M.P., Mr. Francis Noël Baker, president of the British-Hellenic League.

— The texts of the reports both of the British MPs and the International Red Cross Committee and particularly of the latter—owing to unquestionable prestige and well-known objectivity—refuted the slanders one by one and proved:

(1) That no tortures have been inflicted.

(2) That living conditions of deportees are satisfactory.

Of course, during the first weeks of the Revolution, living conditions on Yaros were in no way comfortable. No one has maintained the contrary. The Revolution had to face urgent problems at that time. At all events, from the reports of the International Red Cross Committee, the clear conclusion may be drawn that the living conditions of deportees have never been as described by communist propaganda.

As regards tortures, it has been ascertained by objective investigators, but also by those who made the charges themselves that, in substance, there have been no tortures in any of the places where it has been denounced that these had been inflicted. In addition, it has been proved that, instead of the revolting details mentioned in the report of "Amnesty International", the tortures were confined by the allegedly tortured, only to the torment of *"falanga"*, which has been proved in no case. Moreover, by curious coincidence, the few who have denounced to the International Red Cross that they have been tortured were all active communists with a heavy criminal past.

Statement by George Papadopoulos, Prime Minister of Greece, Minister of National Defense, Minister of Education.

Mr. Gus Yatron, a U.S. Congressman from Pennsylvania, asked the Prime Minister about torture in Greece, adding that on his visit to Greece he had spoken with many people and was personally convinced that it was not true. [From "A Transcription of the August 22, 1969, meeting between Mr. George Papadopoulos, the Prime Minister of Greece, and U.S. Senators and Representatives." Press Office of the Prime Minister of Greece.]

"MR. PAPADOPOULOS: Because of my utter inability to provide you with proofs to the contrary at the moment, allow me to make use of my past status, and speak to you now as the officer I was for a long period of my life. As you know, we officers have no other means of bearing witness to the truth of a position we hold except by giving our word of military honor, which is closely connected to the Church and the Flag.

I therefore assure you, on my word of military honor, which I still hold although I have parted with the glorious uniform, that whatever has been stated as regards tortures is so infuriatingly and basely false, that, in indignation, we often wonder if mankind has not fallen into complete decline, when some people in the Free World so much as discuss the fact that such things might be true of a free people—not to say of Greeks.

I am unfortunately unable to give you any further proof. What I have just said, however, gives the gentleman the right to put me to death by forcing me to suicide—for if he supplies evidence of even one such case as having taken place under the direction of the present regime, then the only duty left to me as a man under solemn military oath, is to commit suicide."

APPENDICES

TORTURE METHODS

The Greek authorities use interrogation techniques that range from simple questioning to torturing to death. The purpose of this Appendix is to give a brief summary of some of the methods used.

Though the *Asphalia* likes to call its torture methods "scientific," they are based mainly on brute force. These methods have proved themselves, and the use of modern methods such as electroshock is generally reserved for particularly recalcitrant or momentarily important prisoners. There are certain objective factors which determine the kinds of torture used. The junta's sensitivity to foreign concern has necessitated the use of techniques that do not leave permanent marks. The economic factor also plays a role. The brutal physical methods tend to be cheaper and simpler than machines and drugs. [Since the summer of 1969 there has been increased use of "truth drugs." According to one source, torture is not so cheap, as the torturers are paid double their normal salary and receive fifteen dollars as a bonus for each name extracted.] They are, to borrow an economist's phrase, "labor intensive." Time is generally an important factor in the choice of methods. The Greek torturers have neither the years of the Soviets to "brainwash" a prisoner for a show trial, nor are they limited to hours the way the French were in Algeria when they caught a man who had placed a bomb. In Greece heresy trials are on a very crude level intellectually, and the resistance has not yet used terror as a weapon. In general they have weeks to work on a prisoner.

Arrests

Arrests are generally carried out between midnight and dawn. The number of arresting officers can range from three to thirty. They have no obligation to identify themselves, nor to have an arrest or search warrant. They generally make a very thorough and often destructive search of the arrested person's house. They do not limit themselves to confiscating what might be relevant to a political investigation such as pamphlets, mimeograph machines, and typewriters. Books, radios, phonographs, tape recorders, toasters, records, and other personal belongings that please the searchers are permanently confiscated.

People are generally roughed up upon arrest. Most are beaten in the car on the way to the police station or army camp. This frightens them and makes them more "receptive" to the interrogation which is to come.

"Civilized" Methods

The *Asphalia* distinguishes between "civilized" methods and "scientific" methods. [Torturers at the Bouboulinas Street *Asphalia,* the so-called "Machine of Truth," have referred to the two methods in these terms.] An arrested person is generally given the opportunity to confess or divulge information by answering questions. This kind of interrogation uses the normal textbook methods. The police know everything ("the jig is up"); the prisoner just has to say it as a formality. The device of a "bad guy" and then a "good guy" in whom the arrested person can confide ("Listen, I'll get in trouble for talking to you, but for your own good, you should. . . .)

The main effort is directed towards making the prisoner feel that it is futile to resist. All the elements in his daily life which give him security are taken away. A reasonable human contact is no longer possible, and the prisoner is frightened and exhausted. He is made to see that no one can help him. Politically no power can change the current situation. The laws under the court martials are "our servants." International organizations such as the Red Cross are ridiculous and powerless. "Everyone talks here," sooner or later, and it would be better for all concerned sooner. Even though these methods might resemble psychologically those employed by all police forces, the fact that the Greek authorities can hold a prisoner incommunicado until he speaks, and the fact he knows they can torture him, places pressures on the prisoner that would not be there under constitutional conditions.

Verbal Methods

From the very first moment the prisoner is verbally assaulted by obscenities, lies, and threats. It is a verbal aggression to which he cannot profitably retaliate. There is the constant use of obscenities and vulgarities. There are political insults, calling a prisoner a "Bulgarian," a "traitor," "Communist." There is a steady stream of lies, lies about the man's family, lies about the man to the family. There are lies about others in his resistance group. In short, all the verbal rules that the culture respects are shattered.

The affidavits generally refer genteely to "horrible insults," "the worst epithets in the Greek language," etc. The following constitutes a typical sample used by the *Asphalia.*

"Hey, boy, how is it with a mother who is a whore?"

"What about his wife, you should see her, she blows everybody of X street."

"We'll bring them both here and fuck them, he'd like watching."

"He's such a fairy he'll really enjoy that."

"What's the matter, fairy, aren't you a man? You don't say anything when someone insults your wife? You know it's true, that's it?"

Threats

From the first moment, threats are directed at the arrested person. If he does not talk he will be killed. Reported threats include death by shooting, stabbing, beating, drowning, poisoning, impalement, defenestration, etc., as well as threats of mutilation, disease, torture, castration, rape, burning, etc. Threats are directed against persons close to the prisoner. Members of the family are threatened with torture, rape, etc., in his presence or they will be brought to watch him being tortured. Often relatives are brought to exercise psychological and moral pressure to make the person give in to the threats.

If these methods fail and the interrogators believe the person has something to reveal, they use physical torture.

Physical Tortures

1. *Beating* The great bulk of the torture is done by a human agent beating the victim. The man doing the beating uses everything from his hands, fists, and feet to such instruments as whips, logs, guns, metal cables, steel rods, rubber truncheons, and boards full of nails. The most commonly used form of physical torture is the *falanga*. Though it generally leaves no permanent scars or disability, it achieves the maximum pain over an extended period of full consciousness. The victim is beaten on the soles of the feet. There are local variations: in Piraeus the victim sits while his feet are thrust through a second chair; in Salonika he is trussed up in a rifle sling; and at Bouboulinas Street he is strapped tightly to a bench worn smooth and shiny by use. [The torturers at Bouboulinas St. have developed a special jargon to describe all their methods. "Pistachios" means, for example, "10 pistachios" means ten *falanga* blows. In Piraeus the torture rooms are called "operating theaters" and the chief torturer is always referred to as "Doctor," never by his real name Yanoutsos.] Generally the shoes are left on to retard swelling, for unimpeded swelling tends to diminish the sensations of the feet. Falanga may continue for hours, the torturers taking turns. In general the victim is forced to walk between rounds, often on a wet floor to restore sensation to the numb feet.

There are variations on what is done while this torture is being performed. At the *Asphalia* in Bouboulinas Street they have a standard escalation of intensity. They start the *falanga* with a wooden stick, then escalate to metal. While the victim is in this position, they can beat him on all the exposed bones and joints. They also beat the genital organs when the victim is in this position. Because the Bouboulinas Street station has the special problem of being in the city, cries are drowned with the noise of a motor or by stuffing a urine-soaked rag down the victim's throat. This and the technique of pouring water down his throat when he screams makes the prisoner feel he is suffocating.

This torture all takes physical effort and involvement on the part of the torturer. It is tiring, and unlike torture by electric shock, the tortured person has a sense of contest, a hope that they cannot go on forever. Physical beating nevertheless remains the most popular method. There are thousands of Greek citizens who have been beaten to differing degrees by either one person or the more usual five to ten or, when forced to run the gantlet at Dionysos, by as many as two hundred soldiers.

2. *Apparatus* The system of electroshock is used in some torture centers. The victim generally has the electrodes attached to sensitive areas of the body such as the feet, the hands, the neck, the genitals. This torture is usually carried out either by doctors or under medical supervision.

Headclamp or headscrew devices have been reported, most notably from Piraeus, where the victim has a steel ring clamped on his head and progressively tightened. One headscrew device is described which also has special clamps for squeezing the ears.

The *Asphalia* of Bouboulinas Street has a device on which the victim is made to sit, and water at high pressure is driven up the anus into the intestines.

The Asphalia of Piraeus, when it had difficulty breaking down Christos Papayiannakis, installed a deafeningly loud bell just outside his telephone-booth-sized cell and rang it at irregular intervals night and day.

3. *Burning* Victims have reported being burned with cigarettes on the thigh, hands, breasts, lips, and arms, being burned on the face with a hot iron and having their facial hair burned off.

4. *Hanging* From many torture places the technique of hanging up a victim for long hours is reported. Men are hung by the arms or by the feet from ceilings or trees. In some camps the victim is handcuffed with his hands behind his back and hung for hours by the handcuffs. They are often beaten while hung up this way, with the result that dislocation of the shoulders may occur.

5. *Sexually oriented tortures* Though there have been no first-hand accounts of rape, much of the tortures used has a definite sexual orientation. This reflects the clearly psychotic character of many of the torturers, such as the Bouboulinas Street specialist, Gravaritis, who spits on men's genitals as he beats them. All kinds of violence are directed against sexual organs. Male genitals are beaten with a braided steel whip and thin sand bags; they are tied with a rope and yanked. Women suffer flogging of the breasts, hitting inferior and superior surfaces of the breasts in rapid succession with a plank, beating in the crotch, and jamming objects such as sticks, guns, or fingers into the vagina. This can have not only a physical but also a strong psychic effect. One young girl in the *Asphalia* was deflowered by a stick and hung from it and another support on the wall. After this she was in a state of shock, unable to respond to any outside stimulus except by tears.

6. *Chemical Agents* Detergent ("Tide") is put in the victim's eyes, mouth, and nose. He may be given chlorine when he asks for water during the tortures. Hot peppers are broken into the victim's mouth and rubbed in sensitive areas. Salt or cigarette ashes are shaken into open wounds.

7. *Miscellaneous* Head and body hair is pulled out, or, alternatively, the hair is shaven off and stuffed into the victim's mouth. In Dionysos Military Camp, vicious dogs were set on the victims in their cells. Victims at Dionysos were also left naked outdoors in the winter and hosed with freezing water. A common device is burial up to the mouth for long periods. The victim may be forced to stand at attention or to kneel for as many as twenty-four or thirty hours—until he collapses. Karate and judo methods are used when beating people, and arms and fingers are twisted to the point of fracture. Often prisoners are left for extended periods with handcuffs on their wrists that are to small to start with and eventually cut into the flesh as their arms, and especially their hands, swell grotesquely.

Nonphysical Methods

1. *Noise* Though noise is physical in the sense that loud sounds can be painful, it has a strong psychological effect as well. Noise plays an integral part in the torture repertory of most centers. Loud bells in the Piraeus *Asphalia,* engines outside cells in Salonika, guards beating on steel cell doors and other metal devices, all drain the prisoner's mental and physical resources.

2. *Nakedness* There is a strong taboo about nakedness in Greek culture and stripping a woman in front of policemen or soldiers can have strong effect on the victim. The interrogation and torture of men and women while they are naked deprives them of one more psychological defense.

3. *Exploitation of psychological weaknesses*   Everyone has certain areas where they are vulnerable psychologically. The torturer tries to play on such negative qualities as vanity or such positive qualities as love. Skillfully exploited, these methods can succeed where physical torture fails. A student resisted the *falanga* and other methods, refusing to reveal names. The arresting officers had found a diary and love letters to his fiancée in his apartment. They read these out loud, mocking him, saying that they were going to bring her there and rape her, then send her to the brothel Papadopoulos had set up for the soldiers. He broke down and gave names.

4. *Hearing others being tortured*   Those who have experienced this claim it is worse than being tortured themselves. Being compelled to listen to the screams, cries, and moans of others has caused psychological distress to the point of nervous breakdown.

5. *Mock executions*   These are convincingly staged and often include the participation of a priest and executioners who fire blanks. They are not the only theatrical efforts, however, for frequently a prisoner, left alone for a few minutes, it attacked by a "madman" who is restrained only at the last moment.

6. *Destruction of sense of reality*   Efforts are sometimes made to convince a victim of torture that he is insane, has only imagined his experiences, and his bruises and injuries are the result of an accident. In other cases a deliberate scheme is adopted to drive a prisoner mad. Aside from the usual deprivations, humiliation, and pain he must suffer, he will be told that it is nighttime at noon, or that there is no man in the room when he sees someone right in front of his eyes. Nervous breakdowns are very common among those who have been tortured, which is not surprising, as torture by its very nature drives mind and body beyond their natural limits.

7. *Signing*   Signing is one of the most devastating methods used by the authorities. As one prisoner said, "You are either arrested and destroyed physically by torture and imprisonment, or you are arrested and destroyed morally by signing." Once in the hands of the authorities it is a rare person who emerges unscathed. Signing is a moral issue, a question of conscience. Those who are the most principled are the ones who suffer the most when they succumb. The ordeal with pen and paper, always accompanied by pressures and threats—and by torture when these are ineffective, begins by the interrogator asking the prisoner to fill out a curriculum vitae. Then he asks for a simple declaration that the man is not a communist, and in a case when he is not might add that there is surely no reason not to write the truth. Then comes the request to condemn the Greek Communist Party, KKE, then the EDA, the left-wing parliamentary party that was legal before the coup, then various liberal organizations, then the man's own activities, friends, and family. Finally, if he has yielded under the psychological and physical torment, he writes a declaration of support for the junta. [Some examples of short declarations, which then appear in the local press, are:

"I condemn the Communist Party of Greece and its offshoots as treasonable and un-Greek and support the National Government."

"As a Greek I condemn such organizations for un-Greek activities and I support unreservedly the National Government."

"At the referendum, I voted for the new Constitution because I believe in the Revolution of 21 April, 1967, and I praise its creative work."]

Men have emerged utterly defeated from this experience which robs them of all self-respect and dignity.

Conditions of Detention

In certain cases the conditions of detention can be considered a form of torture. Prisoners are deprived of food, water, and sleep. Locked in filthy, verminous, solitary confinement cells, they are not allowed to use the toilet. In some detention places the floors of the unfurnished cells are deliberately kept wet and in others sewage overflows unimpeded into the cells. Some cells are so small or so crowded that the person cannot lie down. Prisoners are frequently without blankets or adequate clothing to protect themselves from the bare cement floor, even when it is cold and damp. There is no ventilation. In some cases there is no light, either natural or artificial. There is no competent medical care in the event of sickness.

The Aftereffects of Torture

Those who are tortured will never be the same again. A recent study by Norwegian doctors gives depressing and tragic clinical evidence of the devastating effects of torture. [Axel Strom, M.D.: *Norwegian Concentration Camp Survivors.*] A team of specialists began the study in 1957 of 227 individuals who had been political prisoners during the Second World War. One hundred twenty-four of them had been systematically tortured. The tortures were similar to those described above— blows to the head, burns, traumatic dislocations, etc. The men and women studied were young when they were tortured, just like the majority of Greek victims today. Most of the ex-prisoners said their health had improved after their release, but then began to deteriorate.

Before they were detained, only ten subjects of the study had shown any sign of mental illness. At the time they were examined, 225 out of 227 showed some type of psychic deviation. "The symptoms of these were sleep disturbances and nightmares. Eighty-nine per cent were mostly unstable and often severely depressed. Impotency was strikingly frequent in the age group forty-five to sixty years. Twenty-two per cent had misused drugs or alcohol during the war years. These findings demonstrate that the latent effects of deprivation and torture are as real and serious as the immediate effects. Further deterioration can also be expected." [Howard A. Rusk, M.D.: "Aftermath of Torture," *The New York Times,* July 7, 1968.]

PLACES OF TORTURE AND NAMES OF TORTURERS

The following list includes the places of torture and the names of torturers known to this writer through documents and personal interviews with torture victims. Though the major torture places and leading torturers are probably included, the list no doubt covers only a small proportion of the total. Information generally covers only the major urban areas, and even this is incomplete.

I. The Athens Area
  A. *Asphalia,* Bouboulinas Street, Athens
     (Papaspyropoulos, General Director)
       1. Lambrou, Chief Inspector
       2. Babalis
       3. Christakis
       4. Christaras
       5. Georgiou, Permanent Adjutant
       6. Georgiades
       7. Grammopoulos
       8. Gravaritis
       9. Kalyvas
      10. Karapanayiotis
      11. Karathanassis
      12. Kleomenis
      13. Kontogeorgakis
      14. Leonidas
      15. Logothetis
      16. Mallios
      17. Martinos
      18. Panagopoulos
      19. Papagelis
      20. Spanos
      21. Stefos
      22. Tzavelas
      23. Vlassis
      24. Yiannomitros
  B. Military Hospital 401, Vasilissis Sofias Avenue, Athens
      25. Dr. Karagounakis, Director General
  C. Police Station #5, Hippocratous
  D. Police Station, Perissos
  E. Police Station, Kypseli
      26. Panagopoulos, Director of Asphalia, Kypseli
  F. Police Station, Nea Ionia
      27. Favatas, Major (Police Force)
      28. Karabatsos, Lt. Col. (Police Force, the Commander)
      29. Kollias
      30. Kontoyiorgos, Lt.
      31. Kotiridis
      32. Mavroidis, Lt. Col. (Police Force)
      33. Moroyiannis, Capt. (Police Force)
      34. Rigalas
  G. Police Station, Nea Liosia
  H. Police Station, Kalogreza
  I. Police Station, Aegaleo, St. Spyridon
      35. Zagournas
      36. Kapoyiannis
  J. Police Station, Neo Psychiko
  K. Dionysos Military Camp (505th Battalion)
     (Papadopoulos, Costas, Col. *de facto* commander)
     Manoussakakis, I., Major, Commander of the 505th Battalion
      37. Ioannidis, Vassilis, Lt. Col.
      38. Antonakopoulos

39. Boufas, Con., Major
40. Dogas
41. Koutras, Major
42. Kritikos, Captain
43. Mavromatis, Sub-Lt.
44. Nikolakopoulos
45. Paradias
46. "Pavlos", Military Police (ESA)
47. Peras
48. Seitanidis, Adjutant
49. Sideropoulos, Officer Candidate
50. Spyropoulos, Captain
51. Taxiarchis, Sgt., Military Police (ESA)
52. Theodoracopoulos
53. Theofiloyiannakos, Major
54. Visaniaris, Officer Candidate

L. Agia Paraskevi
55. Zourelis (KYP)
56. Avaliotis, Major
57. Dertilis, Lt. Col.
58. Theofiloyiannakos, Major (same as No. 53)

M. Kessariani, Damari Stone Quarry
59. Lambrou, Basil (same as No. 1)

II. The Piraeus Area

A. *Asphalia,* 37 King Constantine Street, Piraeus
60. Yiannakopoulos, Director, Asphalia
61. Kouvas, Sotirios, Vice-Director
62. Angelopoulos, Panayiotis
63. "Andrikos"
64. Boutos
65. Fotinos
66. Gaveras
67. Iliopoulos
68. Kanatas
69. Karayiannopoulos, D.
70. Kontopyrgias, Sub-Lt.
71. Kotsalos
72. Koutakos
73. Laroutsos, Loukas
74. Sasoulas
75. Tassopoulos
76. Yiannoutsos

B. Karaiskakis Camp

C. Police Station, Kastella

D. Greek Royal Naval Vessel "Elli"
(Lt. Commander Thrasyvoulos Kamarineas, Commander)
77. Kiossos, Nicolaos, Lt.
78. Somaripas, Emmanuel, Warrant Officer
79. Tsipouridis, Nicolaos, Warrant Officer
80. Theofiloyiannakos, Major (same as No. 53)

III. The Salonika Area

A. *Asphalia,* Vardariou Square, Salonika
81. Major Stamatopoulos, Director, Asphalia, Salonika
82. Economou
83. Lepeniotis

84. Stamatelopoulos
85. Varelas
B. Third Army Corps
86. Karamitsos
87. Kourkoulakos, Capt. (KYP)
88. Mestromaras
89. Mitsou
90. Tetradakos
C. KYP, Kalamaria
91. Kourkoulakos (same as No. 86)
92. Papaconstantinos, Anastassios, Colonel
D. Military Airport, 561st Battalion, Sedes
E. Karabournaki Military Camp
F. Emvolon, KYP
G. Lake St. Basil
H. K.E.S.A., (Greek Military Police Center)
93. Papageorgiou, Major, Commandant
I. Military Jail, Eptapyrgion
(Lt. Col. Nicolaos Kavotzimas, Commandant of Camp)
(Lt. Col. Gournizakis)
94. Barbastathis, Nicolaos, Officer Candidate
95. Chrysochou, Georgios
96. Kalaitzidis, Iordanis
97. Karavas, Kostas
98. Mihailidis, Kyriakos
99. Trigiris, Panayiotis
100. Tsakalidis, Konstantinos
101. Tsandas, Nicolaos, Officer Candidate
102. Tsilivarakos, Dimosthenis
103. Tsongas, Nicolaos, Sergeant
104. Typos, Nicolaos
J. Vassilika
105. Christopoolos, Panayiotis, Adjutant
106. Foumas, Hryssanthos

IV. The Patras Area
A. Patras
107. Syfantos, An., Director of Asphalia, Patras
108. Adamopoulos, Georgios
109. Adamopoulos, Laios
110. Michalis
111. Moutsopoulos
112. Papadopoulos
113. Kanellos
114. Tsamis, Dimitrios
V. Agrinion, *Asphalia*
115. Loukopoulos, Sub-Lt.
116. Pengas, Sub-Lt.
117. Spiliopoulos, Sub-Lt.
VI. Corinth
A. Corinth Military Camp
VII. Crete
A. *Asphalia*, Heraklion
118. Koletis, Inspector, Director of Heraklion Asphalia

119. Pechinakis, Deputy Director of Police
120. Choulakis, Officer Candidate
121. Kakkavas
122. Kampasis, Lt. Col.
123. Kapenekou
124. Trouchalakis, Sgt.
B. *Asphalia*, Chania
125. Kapellou
126. Yiorgopoulos

LIST OF TORTURED PERSONS

This list of torture victims has been drawn up from diverse documents such as affidavits, depositions, court declarations, and letters. Some names on this list are based on secondhand evidence. Given the current situation in which those who provide information on torture may be subject to reprisals, it is important to point out that those still in Greece who appear on this list and are now out of prison did not contribute their own names. Their names have been given by those who were witnesses to their torture, or to their condition, or heard them recount their experience. (Some names known abroad have not been placed on this list, in order to protect these people.)

This list has been put together with the greatest possible care. However, in view of the difficult circumstances, there may be errors in details such as profession, place of torture, or place of detention. This list should be thought of as a useful working document for any person, organization, or government making an investigation on this subject. [PD = Place of Detention; PT = Place of Torture.]

1. Aivaliotis, Panayiotis — PD: Laki, Leros
2. Akritidis, Panayiotis — PD: Laki, Leros
3. Alepidis, Evangelos — PD: Averoff Prison
4. Almetidou, Zoi — PT: *Asphalia*, Salonika
5. Ampatielos, Nicos — Accountant
   PT: *Asphalia*, Piraeus
   PD: Partheni, Leros
6. Anagnostopoulos, Byron — Lawyer
   PT: *Asphalia*, Salonika
7. Anagnostopoulou, Helena — PT: *Asphalia*, Bouboulinas St., Athens
8. Anastassiadis, Georgios
9. Anastassiadis, Manolis — Student (University of Hamburg)
   PT: *Asphalia*, Bouboulinas St., Athens
   Asphalia, Piraeus
10. Andritsopoulos, K.
11. Angelaki, Maria — Student
    PT: Nea Ionia Gendarmerie
12. Angelis, Asteris — PD: Averoff Prison
13. Angelidis, Sergios — Student (Athens Polytechnical School)
    PT: *Asphalia*, Bouboulinas St., Athens

14. Angelopoulos, Christos   Student (Athens Polytechnical School)
PT: *Asphalia,* Bouboulinas St., Athens
Corinth Military Camp

15. Angelopoulos, Dimitrios   PD: Laki, Leros

16. Apanomeritakis, Nikolaos   Civil servant
PT: *Asphalia,* Nea Ionia

17. Apelidis, Vassilios   PT: Salonika
PD: Aegina Prison

18. Apolonatos, Evangelos   PD: Averoff Prison

19. Apostolou, Dimitra   PT: Piraeus
PD: Averoff Prison

20. Arapis, Telis   PT: *Asphalia,* Piraeus

21. Arkas, Antonios   PT: Bouboulinas St.
PD: Laki Leros

22. Armaos, Nicolaos   PT: *Asphalia,* Bouboulinas St., Athens
PD: Averoff Prison

23. Arseni, Katerina   Actress
PT: *Asphalia,* Bouboulinas St., Athens
PD: Averoff Prison

24. Athanassiadis, Sotirios   Theater Director
PT: *Asphalia,* Bouboulinas St., Athens
PD: Averoff Prison

25. Athanassiou, Athanassios   Student of Economics
PT: *Asphalia,* Bouboulinas St., Athens
PD: Averoff Prison

26. "Babis"   PT: Salonika, 5th Police Station

27. Bacnrabas, Nondas   PT: Agrinion
PD: Aegina Prison

28. Bakalis, Fotis

29. Balomenos, Christos   Student
PT: *Asphalia,* Bouboulinas St., Athens

30. Balomenòs, Vassilis   PT: Peristeri

31. Banoussis, Themis   Student
PT: *Asphalia,* Bouboulinas St., Athens
PD: Laki, Leros

32. Baras, Argyris   Farmer
PT: Salonika Military Camp
PD: Eptapyrgion Prison, Salonika

33. Bazigos, Georgios   PD: Laki, Leros

34. Bekrodimitri, Katerina   PT: *Asphalia,* Salonika

35. Bekrodimitris, Vassilios   PT: *Asphalia,* Salonika (victim reportedly died)

36. Benas, Takis

37. Bentzelos, Ilias   PT: *Asphalia,* Bouboulinas St., Athens

38. Berdembes, Andreas   Engineer
PT: Karaiskakis Camp
PD: Partheni, Leros

39. Bertsas, Nicolaos   PT: *Asphalia,* Bouboulinas St., Athens

40. Bobas, Harilaos
41. Bomonis, Miltiadis

42. Bonedoukis, Georgios
43. Brillakis, Pavlos
44. Chaidemenos, Epaminondas
45. Chryssikos, Demis

46. Chrissimos, Constantinos

47. Christodoulos, Christos

48. Christodoulou, Maria
49. Christopoulou, Vassiliki

50. Dakos, Apostolos

51. Damalides, Dimitrios
52. Damianakis, Georgios

53. Damigos, Antonis

54. Dariotis, Dimitrios

55. Delaportas, Theodoros
56. Diakakis, G.
57. Diakroussis, Dionysos
58. Diavolakos, Stelios
59. Dimitrelis, Stavros

60. Dimitriou, Petros

61. Dionyssiou, Stamatios
62. Ditsas, Petros

63. Dolkas, Haralambos

64. Dollopoulos, Christos

65. Doukas, Nikos

66. Doulgerakis, Michalis

67. Doulopoulos, Konstantinos
68. Doumas, Panayiotis
69. Douros, Basilios

PD: Laki, Leros
PT: Karaiskakis Camp
PD: Partheni, Leros
PD: Laki, Leros
PT: *Asphalia*, Chania, Crete

Student
PT: *Asphalia*, Bouboulinas St.,
    Athens
PT: Karaiskakis Camp
PD: Laki, Leros
Worker
PT: *Asphalia*, Salonika
PD: Eptapyrgion Prison, Salonika
PT: *Asphalia*, Salonika
Housewife
PT: *Asphalia*, Piraeus
Accountant
PT: *Asphalia*, Bouboulinas, St.,
    Athens
PT: KYP, Salonika
Soldier
PT: ESA (Military Police)
Student
PT: *Asphalia*, Bouboulinas St.,
    Athens
Student (Physics and Mathematics)
PT: *Asphalia*, Bouboulinas St.,
    Athens
PD: Averoff Prison

Doctor

Shoemaker
PT: Gendarmerie
Medical Student
PT: *Asphalia*, Bouboulinas St.,
    Athens
PD: Laki, Leros
Student, Polytechnic School
PT: *Asphalia*, Bouboulinas St.,
    Athens
Student, Polytechnic School
PT: *Asphalia*, Bouboulinas St.,
    Athens
PT: *Asphalia*, Bouboulinas St.,
    Athens
Student
PT: *Asphalia*, Bouboulinas St.,
    Athens
Soldier
PT: ESA (Military Police)
    Nea Ionia Gendarmerie
PD: Laki, Leros

PT: *Asphalia*, Bouboulinas St.,
    Athens
PD: Averoff Prison

70. Doumi, Eleni	PT: Nea Ionia and Villa at Kifissia
71. Dragas, Adam	PD: Eptapyrgion Prison, Salonika
72. Elephtherides, Georgios	PD: Aegina
73. Ellis, Panayiotis	PT: Faliron
74. Eustathiou, I.	
75. Ekaterinakis, Nikos	PT: *Asphalia*, Salonika
76. Exindavelonis, Dimitrios	PT: *Asphalia*, Bouboulinas St., Athens
	PD: Aegina Prison
77. Fandopoulos, Yiannis	PD: Lakı, Leros
78. Farakos, Grigorios	Politician
	PT: *Asphalia*, Bouboulinas St., Athens
	PD: Averoff Prison
79. Felekis, Yiannis	Lithographer
80. Finikides, Dimitrios	PT: Salonika
81. Fitsianos, Andonis	Student
	PT: Peristeri
	Asphalia, Bouboulinas St., Athens
82. Flambouraris, Alecos	Student
	PT: *Asphalia*, Salonika
83. Frangoulakis, Dimitrios	PD: Averoff Prison
84. Frantzeskakıs, Costas	Accountant
	PT: *Asphalia*, Piraeus
	PD: Partheni, Leros; Averoff Prison
85. Follopoulos	Former mayor of Peristeri
86. Gaganiaras, Alekos	Accountant
	PT: Army camp, Salonika
	PD: Eptapyrgion Prison, Salonika
87. Gagarelos, G.	PT: *Asphalia*, Bouboulinas St., Athens
88. Gallos	PD: Laki, Leros
89. Galpinos, Christos	PD: Laki, Leros
90. Gavala, Kallitsa	PT: Salonika Military Camp
91. Gavalas, Petros	Priest
	PT: Crete
92. Gavrilides, Stelios	Student
	PT: *Asphalia*, Bouboulinas St., Athens
93. Gavis, Nicolaos	PD: Laki, Leros
94. Gazis, Antonios	Lawyer
	PT: *Asphalia*, Chania, Crete
95. Gazis, Philippos	PT: *Asphalia*, Chania, Crete
96. Georgakakos, Haralambos	
97. Georgakopoulou, Alexandra	
98. Georgakopoulou, N.	
99. Georgiadou, (female)	PT: Salonika
100. Georgiou, Pelagia	
101. Georgopoulos, Mitsos	PT: Karaiskakis Camp
102. Georgoulas, Babis	Student
	PT: Nea Ionia Gendarmerie
103. Gerali, Maria	Student
	PT: *Asphalia*, Bouboulinas St., Athens
	Dionysos Military Camp

104. Geredakis, Costas — Student
PT: *Asphalia*, Salonika
105. Gitopoulos, Manolis — Business Consultant
PT: *Asphalia*, Salonika
106. Gionoudis, Apostolos — PT: Vassilika, Salonika
107. Gleridis, Michalis — PT: Military Camp, Salonika
108. Glinos, Georgios — Student
PT: *Asphalia*, Bouboulinas St.,
Athens
109. Gogolis, Nicolaos — PT: *Asphalia*, Bouboulinas St.,
Athens
110. Gontikas, Dimitrios — PD: Laki, Leros
111. Grigoriadis, Yiannis — Student (Mathematics)
PD: Eptapyrgion Prison, Salonika
112. Grivas, Cleanthis — Student
PT: *Asphalia*, Bouboulinas St.,
Athens
113. Haitas, Theophilos — PD: Laki, Leros
114. Haralambous, Miltiadis — House painter
PT: *Asphalia*, Bouboulinas St.,
Athens
115. Haralambopoulos, Christos — First Lieutenant
PT: Dionysos Military Camp
PD: Korydallos
116. Harmanidis, Philippos — PT: Fifth Police Station
(Hippocratous)
117. Hatzilouka, Soula — PT: *Asphalia*, Bouboulinas St.,
Athens
118. Hatzis, Georgios — Student
PT: *Asphalia*, Bouboulinas St.,
Athens
119. Hatzivassiliadis
120. Hatziyiannis, Ferdinandos — Student (Industrial School)
PT: Military Camp, Salonika
121. Ikonomidou, Lambrini — PT: Nea Ionia and Perissos
PD: Averoff Prison
122. Iliadis, D.
123. Iliadis, Theodoros — Merchant
PT: *Asphalia*, Piraeus
124. Ioakimidis, Stefanos — Engineer
PT: Third Army Corps, Salonika
125. Ioannidis, Phoebos — Lawyer
PT: *Asphalia*, Heraklion
126. Ioannidou, Elli — Dentist
PT: *Asphalia*, Bouboulinas St.,
Athens
127. Ioannou Yiannis
128. Iordanakis, Grigorios — PD: Laki, Leros
129. Iossifidis, Alexandros — Lawyer, Borough Councillor of
Salonika
PT: Salonika, Third Army Corps
and Asphalia
130. Issakidis, Georgios — PT: *Asphalia*, Salonika
131. Kaklamanos, Theodoros — PT: Karaiskakis Camp
132. Kakis, Georgia — PT: Chania, Crete
133. Kalaitzis, Theodoros — PT: Peristeri
Asphalia Bouboulinas St.,
Athens

134. Kalanzandonakis, Michalis   PT: Chania, Crete
135. Kalatzis, Charalambos   Merchant
PT: Aegaleo, Agios Spyridon
     Police Station
136. Kallergi, Maria   Student (Mathematics)
PT: *Asphalia*, Bouboulinas St.,
     Athens
     Dionysos Military Camp
PD: Averoff Prison
137. Kalfakakos, Panayiotis   PD: Laki, Leros
138. Kallipolitis, Charalambos
139. Kalogeropoulos, Kimon   PT: *Asphalia*, Bouboulinas St.,
     Athens
140. Kalogridis, Stavros   PD: Laki, Leros
141. Kanellopoulos, Athanassios   Employee, Telecommunications
PT: *Asphalia*, Piraeus
142. Kanellis, Eleftherios   PD: Averoff Prison
143. Kamari, Popi   Student (Philosophy)
PT: *Asphalia*, Bouboulinas St.,
     Athens
     Asphalia, Piraeus
PD: Averoff Prison
144. Kapetanakis, Dimitris   Student
PT: *Asphalia*, Salonika
145. Kara, Aspasia   Teacher (Greek Literature)
Borough Councillor of Salonika
PT: Salonika, Third Army Corps
146. Karageorgas, Dionyssios   Professor (Public Finance)
PT: Aretaieion Hospital, Athens
     (tortured while still wounded
     from bomb explosion)
     Police Station, Nea Ionia
147. Karatsis, Charalambos   PT: Aegaleo
148. Karamitsis, Epaminondas   Stenographer
PT: Gendarmerie
149. Karageorgiou, Triandafyllos   PD: Averoff Prison
150. Karaosman, Bashari   PT: Agia Paraskevi
PD: Psitalia Naval Prison,
     Psitalia Island
151. Karantinos, Panayiotis   PT: *Asphalia*, Bouboulinas St.,
     Athens
152. Karavitis, Panos   PT: Piraeus, Asphalia
PD: Partheni, Leros
153. Karayannis   PT: *Asphalia*, Bouboulinas St.,
     Athens
154. Karkiroglou, Corina
155. Karelas, Dimitrios
156. Karelis, Emmanuel   PT: Chania, Crete
157. Karfis, Georgios   Student
PT: Third Army Corps, Salonika
158. Karyotakis, Konstantinos   Student (Pandios School)
PT: *Asphalia*, Bouboulinas St.,
     Athens
159. Karipidis, Georgios   Soldier
PT: Military Camp, Corinth
160. Karouta, Anna   Worker
PT: Nea Ionia suburb police
     station
PD: Averoff Prison

161. Karpetas, Efstratios
162. Karmiris, Dimitrios

163. Karra, Aspasia

164. Kassapidis, Dimitrios

165. Katinakis, Kyriakos
166. Katsavounidis, Eleftherios
167. Katsigra, Kaliopi

168. Katsouras, Haralambos
169. Katsouridou, Evgenia

170. Kazelis, Theodoros

171. Kazos

172. Keramida, Parthena

173. Keramitzis, Nondas
174. Kiaos, Nicolaos

175. Kilakos, Stamatios

176. Kilindris, Anastasios
177. Kimiatzis, Panayiotis
178. Kiritsis, Lazaros

179. Kirkoudis, Yiannis

180. Kissas, Georgios
181. Klavdianos, Pavlos

182. Klonizakis, Yiannis

183. Kokoris

184. Kokou, Eleftheria
185. Koliarakis, Dimitrios

186. Kolovos, Lefteris
187. Koliviras

PD: Averoff Prison
PT: *Asphalia,* Piraeus
PD: Partheni, Leros
PT: *Asphalia,* Salonika
PD: Eptapyrgion Prison, Salonika
Teacher
PT: *Asphalia,* Piraeus

PD: Laki, Leros
Dressmaker
PT: *Asphalia,* Bouboulinas St.,
    Athens
PD: Averoff Prison
PD: Nea Fylaki, Salonika
Secretary of the Union of
    Telephone Operators
Student (Economics)
PT: Third Army Corps, Salonika
PD: Eptapyrgion Prison, Salonika
Student
PT: *Asphalia,* Bouboulinas St.,
    Athens
PT: Third Army Corps, Salonika
    Second Police Station,
    Salonika

Teacher (Physics, Mathematics)
PT: *Asphalia,* Bouboulinas St.,
    Athens
Student
PT: *Asphalia,* Piraeus
PD: Partheni, Leros
PD: Laki, Leros
PD: Laki, Leros
Lawyer
PT: *Asphalia,* Bouboulinas St.,
    Athens
PD: Averoff Prison
Student (Mathematics)
PT: *Asphalia,* Salonika
PD: Averoff Prison
Student (Commerce)
PT: *Asphalia,* Bouboulinas St.,
    Athens; Dionysos Military
    Camp
PD: Averoff Prison
Civil Engineer
PT: *Asphalia,* Bouboulinas St.,
    Athens
PD: Aegina Prison
Merchant
PT: *Asphalia,* Bouboulinas St.,
    Athens
PD: Averoff Prison
Merchant Navy Engineer
PT: *Asphalia,* Piraeus
PD: Partheni, Leros

PT: Gendarmerie, Nea Ionia

188. Komatas, Petros — Worker
PT: Gendarmerie, Athens
189. Komminos, Nicolaos — PD: Laki, Leros
190. Kompsopoulos, Georgios — PT: Salonika
191. Kondoyiorgos, Christos — Bookseller
PT: *Asphalia*, Bouboulinas St., Athens

192. Konstantakis, Nonis — PT: Salonika
193. Konstantinou, Dora — Student
PT: Piraeus

194. Konstantopoulos, Apostolos — PD: Laki, Leros
195. Konstantopoulos, Donios — PD: Laki, Leros
196. Konstantopoulos, Georgios — PT: Salonika
197. Korbakis, Dimitrios — House painter
PT: Patras

198. Korkoris, Nicolaos — PD: Laki, Leros
199. Korovesis, Perikles — Actor
PT: *Asphalia*, Bouboulinas St., Athens
Military Hospital 401, Athens

200. Kostopoulos, Dimitrios — PT: *Asphalia*, Bouboulinas St., Athens
PD: Averoff Prison Hospital

201. Koukas — Journalist
202. Koutsogeorgas, Aristoteles — PT: *Asphalia*, Bouboulinas St., Athens

203. Koutsoyorgos, Christos — PT: *Asphalia*, Bouboulinas St., Athens

204. Koulganda, Theodora — Student
PT: Salonika

205. Kouridakis, Spyros — PD: Averoff Prison
206. Kousouras, Theoharis — PT: Salonika
207. Kraniotis, Titos
208. Lakidou
209. Lambrianos, Georgios — Deputy of Center Union Party
210. Lambrinakos, Nicos — PT: *Asphalia*, Piraeus
211. Lambrinos, Venediktos — Engineer
PT: Suburban police station

212. Lekanidis, Nicolaos — Employee
PT: *Asphalia*, Bouboulinas St., Athens
PD: Aegina Prison

213. Leloudas, Yiannis — Poet, Archaeologist
PT: *Asphalia*, Bouboulinas St., Athens

214. Lendakis, Andreas — Teacher (Greek literature)
PT: *Asphalia*, Bouboulinas St., Athens
PD: Partheni, Leros

215. Levendakis, Yiannis — Student
PT: *Asphalia*, Salonika

216. Liapi, Frida — Student (Humanities)
PT: *Asphalia*, Bouboulinas St., Athens

217. Lipas, Ioannis — PD: Averoff Prison
218. Lippa, Sofia — PT: *Asphalia*, Piraeus
219. Livanos, Dionysios — Newspaperman
PT: Agia Paraskevi

220. Livanis, Antonis — PT: Heraklion *Asphalia*, Crete

221. Likoudas, Spyros   Law Student
222. Linos   PT: *Asphalia*, Bouboulinas St., Athens
223. Logothetis, Dimos   PT: Cemetery of village of Vassilika, Salonika
224. Loissios, Leon   Film Director
   PT: *Asphalia*, Bouboulinas St., Athens
   Military Police Building, Athens
225. Loupetis, Yiannis   PD: Averoff Prison
226. Malistathis, Pandelis   PT: *Asphalia*, Bouboulinas St., Athens
   PD: Laki, Leros
227. Mallidis, Constantinos   PD: Laki, Leros
228. Malliothanassis, Pandelis   PT: *Asphalia*, Bouboulinas St., Athens
229. Manaziotis, Dimitrios   PD: Laki, Leros
230. Mandeos, Constantinos   Law Student
   PT: *Asphalia*, Bouboulinas St., Athens
231. Mandeos, Nicolaos   Student
232. Mandeos, Petros   Clerk
   PD: Aegina Prison
233. Mangakis, George   Law Professor
   PD: Petroupolis Gendarmerie
234. Manolakas, Aristidis   Student
   PT: *Asphalia*, Bouboulinas St., Athens
   PD: Partheni, Leros
235. Marangoudakis   PD: Chalepas Prison, Chania
236. Maratos
237. Margaritis, Antonis   Student (Athens Agricultural School)
   PT: *Asphalia*, Bouboulinas St., Athens
238. Marissios, Argyris
239. Marketakis, Pandelis   PT: Crete
240. Masmanidis, Artemios   PD: Laki, Leros
241. Mastoras, Vassilis   Engineer
   PT: Third Army Corps, Salonika
   PD: Eptapyrgion Prison, Salonika
242. Matakis   Soldier
   PD: Averoff Prison
243. Mavromatis, Dimos   PT: *Asphalia*, Bouboulinas St., Athens
244. Mavroskoufis, Aristidis (Cypriot)   Student (Physics)
   PT: *Asphalia*, Bouboulinas St., Athens
245. Meletis. Constantine   PT: *Asphalia*, Salonika
246. Mekrodimitris   PT: *Asphalia*, Piraeus
247. Messinis. Eustratios   PT: *Asphalia*, Heraklion
248. Michailidis. Nicolaos   PT: *Asphalia*, Salonika
249. Michaltos. Spyros   PT: *Asphalia*, Piraeus
250. Michelinakis, Yiannis   PT: *Asphalia*, Salonika
251. Michaloyiannis, Georgios   Housepainter
   PT: *Asphalia*, Salonika
   PD: Eptapyrgion Prison, Salonika

252. Miltiadis. Charalambos	PD: Laki, Leros
253. Miltsis. Dimitrios	PD: Laki. Leros
254. Missios, Chronis	PT: *Asphalia*, Piraeus
	Dionysos Military Camp
255. Moraitis, Angelos	Worker
	PT: At the Police Station
256. Moraitis, Georgios	Writer
	PT: *Asphalia*, Bouboulinas St.,
	Athens
257. Moschonas, Panayiotis	Bookseller
	PT: *Asphalia*, Bouboulinas St.,
	Athens
258. Moschos, Christos	PD: Eptapyrgion Prison, Salonika
259. Moschos, Nicolaos	
260. Naskos, Stavros	PD: Nea Fylaki. Salonika
261. Nefeloudis, P.	PD: Averoff Prison
262. Neikos, Christos	PD: Nea Fylaki, Salonika
263. Nestor, Stelios	Lawyer
	PT: *Asphalia*, Salonika
	KYP, Salonika
264. Nikolopoulos, Yiannis	Mechanic
	PT: *Asphalia*, Bouboulinas St.,
	Athens
	PD: Averoff Prison
265. Notaras, Gerassimos	Political Scientist
	PT: *Asphalia*, Bouboulinas St.,
	Athens
	Greek Royal Naval Vessel,
	the "Elli"
	PD: Aegina Prison
266. Ouranos, Georgios	PT: *Asphalia*, Heraklion, Crete
267. Ouzounis, Christos	
268. Papazidis	Borough Councillor of Peristeri
	PT: *Asphalia*, Piraeus
269. Palamaras, Christos	Accountant
	PT: *Asphalia*, Bouboulinas St..
	Athens
270. Paleologos, Constantinos	Petty officer. Navy
	PT: Greek Royal Naval Vessel,
	the "Elli"
271. Panagoulis, Alexandros	Soldier
	PT: *Asphalia*, Bouboulinas St.,
	Athens
	PD: Prison unknown after recent
	escape and recapture
272. Panayiotakopoulos, Thanassis	PT: *Asphalia*, Bouboulinas St.,
	Athens
	PD: Laki, Leros
273. Panayiotidis. Serafim	PD: Laki, Leros
274. Pandis, Gregorios	Tailor
	PT: Third Army Corps, Salonika
	PD: Eptapvrgion Prison, Salonika
275. Pangopoulou. Georgia	PT: *Asphalia*, Salonika
276. Pantazidis, Nikolaos	PT: Piraeus Asphalia
	PD: Averoff Prison
277. Papadakis. Anestis	PT: *Asphalia*, Salonika
278. Papadakis. Emmanuel	PT: Crete
279. Papadimitriou, Litsa	

280. Papadomichalakis, Chariton   Cabinetmaker
  PT: *Asphalia*, Heraklion, Crete
  PD: Averoff Prison
281. Papadopoulos, Costas   PT: Third Army Corps, Salonika
282. Papadopoulos, Sofronios   PD: Averoff Prison
283. Papadopoulos, Tsamis
284. Papadopoulou, Maria   PT: Salonika
285. Papalexiou, Dimitris   PT: Third Army Corps, Salonika
286. Papamichail, Dimitrios   Student, Soldier
  PT: Corinth Military Training
    Camp
287. Papalexis, Alecos   Journalist, ex-deputy
  PT: Third Army Corps, Salonika
  PD: Eptapyrgion Prison, Salonika
288. Papamargaris, Charis   Assistant at University
  PT: Nea Ionia Gendarmerie
289. Papangelou, Sonia   PT: *Asphalia*, Salonika
290. Papanicola, Anna   PT: *Asphalia*, Bouboulinas St.,
    Athens
291. Papanicolaou, Yiannis   Student (Polytechnical School)
  PT: *Asphalia*, Bouboulinas St.,
    Athens
292. Papayiannakis, Christos   Architect's assistant
  PT: *Asphalia*, Piraeus
293. Papayiannakis (sister)   PT: *Asphalia*, Piraeus
294. Papayianneas, Yiannis   Printer
  PT: *Asphalia*, Piraeus
295. Papayiannou, Manolis   PT: Chania, Crete
296. Papazisis   Editor
  PT: Military Police ESA
297. Paraskevas, Nicolaos   Plumber
  PT: Police Station
298. Partazidis, Nicolaos   PD: Averoff Prison
299. Partheni, Maria   PT: *Asphalia*, Salonika
300. Paschalidis, Theodoros   PD: Laki, Leros
301. Patsikou (Mrs.)
302. Pavlopoulos, Evangelos   Bank employee
303. Payiadakos, Petros
304. Pelonis, Constantinos   PD: Laki, Leros
305. Petropoulos, Yiannis   Housepainter
  PT: *Asphalia*, Bouboulinas St.,
    Athens
    Dionysos Military Camp
306. Pitaka, Magda   Nurse
  PT: *Asphalia*, Bouboulinas St.,
    Athens
    Dionysos Military Camp
307. Plazomytis, Constantinos   PD: Laki, Leros
308. Pnevmatikos, Anghelos   Army Officer
  PT: Dionysos Military Camp
  PD: Korydallos
309. Pnevmatikos, Constantinos   Engineer Captain
  PT: Third Army Corps, Salonika
    Agia Paraskevi
  PD: Korydallos
310. Podoras. Gerassimos   PD: Laki, Leros
311. Polydefkis, Melios   Industrialist

312. Politis, Andreas   Petty Officer, Navy
                                 PT: Greek Naval Vessel the "Elli"
                                 PD: Aegina Prison
313. Politis, Nicolaos   Building contractor
                                 PT: *Asphalia*, Bouboulinas St.,
                                      Athens
314. Polovinis, P.   School Inspector
                                 PT: *Asphalia*, Bouboulinas St.,
                                      Athens
315. Polyxenaki, Cleo   PT: *Asphalia*, Bouboulinas St.,
     (Polychronaki?)   Athens
316. Pomonis, Miltiadis   PT: Karaiskaki Camp
317. Protopapas, Charalambos   Solicitor
                                 President of the Democratic
                                      Socialist League, Secretary
                                      of the Greek League of
                                      Human Rights
                                 PT: *Asphalia*, Bouboulinas St.,
                                      Athens
318. Psihoulis, Nicolaos   PD: Averoff Prison
319. Pyrgos, Sotiris   PT: Agrinion
320. Pyrzas, Constantinos   Lecturer in Philosophy, Univ. of
                                      Salonika
                                 PT: KYP, Kalamaria, Salonika
321. Raptis, Polytimos   PD: Laki, Leros
322. Reklitis, Christos   Construction worker
                                 PT: *Asphalia*, Bouboulinas St.,
                                      Athens
                                      Dionysos Military Camp
                                 PD: Averoff Prison
323. Resposidos
324. Rodakis, Pericles   PT: *Asphalia*, Bouboulinas St.,
                                      Athens
325. Rokofylos   PT: Nea Ionia Gendarmerie
326. Sabinis, Dimitrios   Worker
                                 PT: *Asphalia*, Salonika
327. Sakislis, Dimitrios   Student (Athens Polytechnical
                                      School)
328. Sakhpekidis, Antonis   Student
                                 PT: *Asphalia*, Bouboulinas St.,
                                      Athens
329. Sakoulidis, Efthymios   PD: Laki, Leros
330. Salpadimas. K.   PT: *Asphalia*, Piraeus
331. Sapountzi. Afroula   PT: *Asphalia*, Salonika
332. Satiglis, Dimitris
333. Savakis, Andreas   Student (Higher Industrial School)
                                 PT: Crete
                                      Asphalia, Bouboulinas St.
                                      Athens
334. Savinidou, Poli   Student (Architecture)
     (or Penelopi)   PT: *Asphalia*. Piraeus
                                 PD: Averoff Prison
335. Savinidou. Selini   PT: 11th Police Station in Piraeus
336. Sideras, Spyros   Journalist
                                 PT: *Asphalia*, Bouboulinas St.,
                                      Athens
337. Sideris, Agamemnon   PD: Laki, Leros
338. Sideris, Leonidas   Accountant

PT: Police Station, Kypseli
    Asphalia, Bouboulinas St.,
    Athens
PD: Averoff Prison
339. Sideropoulos, Georgios   PT: KYP, Salonika
340. Sipitanos, Georgios   Merchant
                                     PT: Kalamaria, Salonika
                                         KYP, Salonika
                                     PD: Aegina Prison
341. Skarlis, Georgios   PT: Salonika
342. Skartsas, Orestis
343. Skoufakis, Nicos   PT: *Asphalia*, Bouboulinas St.,
                                         Athens
                                     PD: Laki, Leros
344. Smyrni, Sofia   Dressmaker
                                     PT: *Asphalia*, Patras
                                     PD: Averoff Prison
345. Sombolas, Constantinos   PD: Laki, Leros
346. Sotirakos   Student (Commercial School)
                                     PT: *Asphalia*, Bouboulinas St.,
                                         Athens
347. Sofoulis, Constantinos   PT: *Asphalia*, Bouboulinas St.,
                                         Athens
                                     PD: Aegina Prison
348. Sotiriadou, Tassia   Worker
                                     PT: *Asphalia*, Piraeus
                                     PD: Averoff Prison
349. Sotiriou, Nikolaos   PD: Averoff Prison
350. Souvatzoglou, Anestis   PT: *Asphalia*, Bouboulinas St.,
                                         Athens
351. Spyridakis, Michalis   Medical Student
                                     PT: *Asphalia*, Salonika
                                     PD: Eptapyrgion Prison, Salonika
352. Spyridakis, S.
353. Spyridou, Despina
354. Stamatakis, Constantinos   Soldier
                                     PT: E.S.A. (Military Police)
355. Stamatakis, Nikiforos   Employee
                                     PT: *Asphalia*, Heraklion, Crete
                                         Asphalia, Bouboulinas St.,
                                         Athens
356. Stamatopoulou, Sofia   PT: Salonika
357. Stefanidis, Socrates   PT: *Asphalia*, Salonika
                                     PD: Eptapyrgion prison, Salonika
358. Stergiou
359. Strabis   PT: *Asphalia*, Bouboulinas St.,
                                         Athens
360. Stratis, Yiannis   Teacher (Mathematics)
                                     PT: Dionysos Military Camp
                                     PD: Lefkada Prison
361. Svanas, V.   PT: *Asphalia*, Bouboulinas St.,
                                         Athens
362. Taoussianis, Philippos   PT: Vassilika, Salonika
363. Theodorakakos, Michalis   Merchant
                                     PT: *Asphalia*, Piraeus
364. Theodorakakou, Evangelia   PT: *Asphalia*, Piraeus
365. Theodoridis, Anastassios   PD: Laki, Leros
366. Theodoridis, Aristidis   Student (Mathematics)

		PT: *Asphalia*, Bouboulinas St., Athens
367.	Theodoridis, Grigorios	PD: Laki, Leros
368.	Theodorou, Christos	Worker
		PT: *Asphalia*, Bouboulinas St., Athens
369.	Theofylaktopoulou, Evangelia	Student (Decorative Arts)
		PT: *Asphalia*, Bouboulinas St., Athens
370.	Theoharidis, Theoharis	PT: *Asphalia*, Salonika
371.	Thitsas, Petros	
372.	Tholios, Yiannis	Student (Industrial School)
		PT: *Asphalia*, Bouboulinas St., Athens
373.	Thomadakis, Theodosis	PD: Averoff Prison
374.	Thomaris, Tassos	
375.	Toukas, Constantinos	Worker
		PT: Police Station
376.	Triaridis, Constantinos	Doctor
		PT: KYP, Salonika
377.	Trovas, Georgios	PD: Averoff Prison
378.	Tsakarestos, Constantinos	Employee of Post Office
		PT: *Asphalia*, Bouboulinas St., Athens
379.	Tsangarakis, Michalis	PD: Averoff Prison
380.	Tsakiris, Christos	PD: Laki, Leros
381.	Tsakouridou, Eugenia	PT: *Asphalia*, Bouboulinas St., Athens
382.	Tsaroucha, Keti	Farmer's wife
		PT: Salonika
383.	Tselekidis, Yiannis	PT: Salonika
384.	Tsemekidis, Dimitrios	PD: Nea Fylaki
385.	Tsepekidis, Nicos	PT: *Asphalia*, Salonika
386.	Tseremenglis, Panayiotis	PT: Patras 5th Police Station
387.	Tsevelikou, Kalliopi	PT: *Asphalia*, Bouboulinas St., Athens
388.	Tsigounis, Vassilis	PT: *Asphalia*, Piraeus
		PD: Partheni, Leros
389.	Tsiloglou, Eleftherios	Student, Secretary of E.F.E.E. (former National Student Union of Greece)
		PT: *Asphalia*, Bouboulinas St., Athens
		Dionysos Military Camp
		PD: Averoff Prison
390.	Tsimekis, Michalis	PD: Averoff Prison
391.	Tsimikidis, Dimitrios	Tailor
		PT: *Asphalia*, Salonika
		PD: Eptapyrgion Prison, Salonika
	Tsimokis, Michalis	PT: *Asphalia*, Bouboulinas St., Athens
393.	Tsirka, Natassa	Student (English Literature)
		PT: *Asphalia*, Bouboulinas St., Athens
394.	Tsironakis, Constantinos	PD: Laki, Leros
395.	Tsivani, Evangelia	PT: Piraeus
396.	Tsokou, Roi	Athens University Graduate
397.	Tsolakidou, Olga	Hairdresser

398. Tsoris, Kyriakos

399. Tsoutsas, Constantinos
399.
400. Tzavellas, Panayiotis

401. Tzembelikou, Popi

402. Tzonandreou

403. Vardikos, Nikos

404. Varoulis
405. Vassiliou, Nicolaos
406. Vassiliou

407. Veneris, Evangelos
408. Verivakis. Eleftherios
409. Veros, Costas
410. Vlassis, Petros

411. Votsakis, Gerassimos

412. Voulelis, N.

413. Vrentzos, Costas

414. Vrentzos, Haralambos

415. Xarchoulakos, Yiannis

416. Xakoulakos. Yiannis
417. Xiritakis, Demetrios
418. Yakoumatos, Emmanuel
419. Yiannadakis, Nicolaos

420 Yiannoulis, Serafim
421. Yiannopoulos, Georgios
422. Yianogonas, Yiannis
423. Yiotopoulos, Georgios
424. Yiorgos, Costas

425. Yiotopoulos, Manolis
426. Zervopoulos, Ioannis

PT: *Asphalia,* Piraeus
PD: Averoff Prison
PT: *Asphalia,* Bouboulinas St.,
    Athens
Medical Student
PD: Eptapyrgion Prison, Salonika
Musician
PT: Police Station, Athens suburb
Student
PT: *Asphalia,* Bouboulinas St.,
    Athens
    Asphalia, Piraeus
PT: *Asphalia,* Bouboulinas St.,
    Athens
PT: *Asphalia,* Bouboulinas St.,
    Athens

PD: Laki, Leros
Economist
PT: Nea Ionia Gendarmerie

Lawyer

Student
PT: *Asphalia,* Bouboulinas St.,
    Athens
Student (Polytechnical School)
PT: Dionysos Military Camp
    Asphalia, Bouboulinas St.,
    Athens
PT: *Asphalia,* Bouboulinas St.,
    Athens
Student
PT: Military Police, Salonika
Student
PT: Military Police, Salonika
PT: *Asphalia,* St. Spyridon,
    Aegaleo
PD: Aegina Prison
PT: Aegaleo Gendarmerie
PT: Heraklion, Crete
PD: Averoff Prison
Student (Law)
PT: *Asphalia,* Bouboulinas St.,
    Athens
PD: Laki, Leros
PT: *Asphalia,* Heraklion
PD: Laki, Leros
PT: *Asphalia,* Piraeus
Student (Law)
PT: *Asphalia,* Bouboulinas St.,
    Athens
PT: KYP, Salonika
Army Captain

Some Persons Killed by the Authorities

1. Dimopoulos, Yiannis (8 years old)

Killed by E.S.A. after undergoing torture to force him to reveal his father's hiding place, Aegaleo, July 1967.

2. Ellis, Panayiotis

Shot dead, Faliron Stadium April 25, 1967, by 2nd Lt. Constantinos Kotsakis.

3. Halkidis, G.

Shot to death on September 5, 1967, at Salonika.

4. Hassakidis, Zoitsa

Died after being tortured and raped near Salonika at the end of September, 1967.

5. Kalabrou, Maria

Shot to death April 27, 1967, Pattission Street, Athens.

6. Kalyvas, Dimitrios

Infantry Captain, killed on July 7, 1967, after taking a position against the military coup.

7. Konidis, Porfyris

Died as a result of tortures at the Bouboulinas Street *Asphalia* in Athens.

8. Ladas, G.

Killed May 5, 1967, Athens at Tritis Septemvriou st.

9. Mandilaras, Nikiforos

Athenian lawyer, close to the Papandreous, killed off the island of Rhodes shortly after the coup.

10. Mekrodimitris

Labor union official, died in the Piraeus Asphalia in 1967 after having been tortured.

11. Paleologos, Constantinos

Naval Petty Officer who died as a result of torture aboard the "Elli."

12. Tsarouchas, Georgios

Ex-Deputy
Died in May, 1968, after having been beaten by the police outside Salonika.

LIST OF RESISTANCE ORGANIZATIONS

Principal Resistance Organizations

1.	AAMY	Rural Agrarian Front Against Dictatorship
2.	DA	Democratic Defense
3.	EFEE	National Union of Greek Students
4.	MEL	Freedom Front
5.	PAK	Pan-Hellenic Liberation Movement
6.	PAM	Patriotic Front
7.	Rigas Ferraios	Pan-Hellenic Anti-Dictatorial Student Organization

Other Resistance Organizations

This list compiles known illegal and resistance organizations. Some of these organizations such as DEA, DEKA, and EA were important but have been broken up. Others are of little significance. Some are simply offshoots and fronts of other organizations such as PEAA, which is front for the Koliyiannis faction of the Greek Communist Party (KKE). No attempt is made in this list to evaluate the importance of each group.

1.	A	Resistance
2.	AEM	Anti-Dictatorial Workers' Front
3.	AEPA	Workers' Radical Resistance Movement
4.	AEKK	National Freedom Movement of Crete
5.	AKA	Anti-Fascist Greek Movement
6.	DEA	Democratic Resistance Committees
7.	DEKA	Democratic National Resistance Movement
8.	DAS	Democratic Association for Freedom
9.	EE	Free Greeks
10.	EAN	Greek Anti-Dictatorial Youth
11.	EAS	National Anti-Fascist Association
12.	EEE	Greek Nationalist Union
13.	EES	National Union of Salvation (army group)

14. EKA	Greek Resistance Movement
15. EKDA	National Movement of Democratic Resistance
16. EOAA	Organization of Veteran Greek Officers
17. EODA	National Democratic Defense Organization
18. EOE	Greek National Organization
19.	General "Akritas" (army group)
20. KKE	Greek Communist Party (Koliyiannis)
21. KKE	Greek Communist Party (Partsalides)
22. K	The Movement
23. ODA	Democratic Resistance Groups
24. ODEF	Organization of Democratic Greek Students
25. P	Pyrsos (army group)
26. PAS	Pan-Hellenic Anti-Fascist Association
27. PEAA	Pan-Hellenic Committee for the Struggle Against Dictatorship
28. PEA	Panhellenic Committee of Mutual Aid
29. SNA	Association of Young Fighters
30. EA	Greek Resistance
31.	Invisible Fighters of the Greek Nation